PARENT-DRIVEN SCHOOLS

PARENT-DRIVEN SCHOOLS

A Public School Warrior's
Fight to Revolutionize Education

RANDY GASCHLER

Notice

Mention of specific companies, organizations, or authorities in this book does not imply endorsements by the publisher, nor does mention of specific companies, organizations, or authorities in the book imply that they endorse the book.

KELE PUBLISHING
4069 Alice Court
Placerville, CA 95667

For information regarding special discounts for bulk purchases, please contact Kele Publishing Special Sales at 1-530-622-3532 or Kelepublishing.com

Manufactured in the United States of America

10 9 8 7 6 5 4 3 2 1

The Library of Congress Cataloging-in-Publication Data is available
Randy Gaschler
        Parent-Driven Schools: A Public School Warrior's Fight to Revolutionize Education /
Randy Gaschler. – Rev. ed.;1st Kele Publishing ed.
        p.   cm.
        1. Schools—Education—United States 2. Schools—Educational aspects—United States.   I. Title
        DNLM: 1. Education—reform—Popular Works. 2. School—parent-driven—Popular Works. 3. Learning—revolution—Popular Works. 4. Teaching—Popular Works
TXu1-213-199
ISBN 0-9762931-0-2

CONTENTS

PREFACE

If your child's school was run by politicians, and bureaucrats determined what subjects were being taught and parents had no say at all, would you demand changes? If you answered "yes" then this book was written for you.

I wrote it because as a parent, coach, and teacher for most of my adult life, I am convinced that America's system of public education is terribly flawed. I firmly believe that we—you and I and all the other parents and caring people in this country—have the power to fix it. We can change public education. The power lies with us, in our hands, and in our hearts.

For the past decade, I have fought for alternatives in education—for schools and teachers who are accountable directly to parents, not to politicians or administrators. I have designed and run school systems that are based on helping children become lifelong learners. Our schools are built to be flexible so they can serve all children, not just the chosen few who were born with the ability to memorize facts and successfully regurgitate them back on multiple-choice, standardized tests.

I believe that learning should not be punishment for children. I also believe that reading about education should not be punishment for adults. That's why I chose to write this book in an easygoing, anecdotal style. If you are an academic, looking for a long-winded tome on philosophies of education, you are reading the wrong book. The people I want to reach are those who are naturally the most passionate about education—parents and committed educators. Inside these pages, you will find that I have written about my own journey (scars, warts and all), through the deep tangle of California's educational jungle to fight for the changes I feel must be made for our children and our future. The fight has taken us, often reluctantly, into the halls and deep recesses of the state legislature, into the smoky back rooms where deals are cut, and even into the state court system. The encouraging results have been historic new laws that are changing the face of education in California. I'm proud of my role in making that happen. Yet, there is much, much more to do.

It isn't going to be easy. Nationwide, the "educrats" are deeply entrenched and seem to hold all the power—and sometimes they play dirty. But I am either too committed, or too hard-headed to quit. By the end of this book, I hope you will not only understand why these established bureaucrats and unions are terrified of education reform (and the lengths to which they will go to stop it), but more importantly, that the parents in this country can prevail. In the past ten years, I have come to realize that the real power lies with the parents of all of the children in our public school system—if we could only realize how to wield it. For too long, parents throughout America have been led to believe that they have no right to make decisions about their child's education. For too long, we've left it in the hands of politicians and school administrators. The truth is, we not only have the right to change the system, we have the power and the duty. I'm angry about what is being done—and not being done—in our schools. I'm angry that politicians, teachers' unions and administrators have seized iron-fisted control to further their own purposes, and I'm angry that teachers often misunderstand their proper role and are marginalized by the bureaucrats, and that parents have no say at all.

The purpose of the book is to convince you that, together, we can change public education. To the uninitiated, the issues surrounding education can seem bewildering, thickly bureaucratic, and even boring. Yet, as you will read in this book, they are none of these things once you learn a little about them. I have yet to meet a politician who is as persuasive about education as an informed parent. The truth is that taking back our schools and making them accountable to parents is the most important thing we can do in our lives for our children and our future.

Randy Gaschler
Placerville, Ca.

A Favor!

Before we really get going on my favorite subject—fixing our shipwrecked education system—I'd like to ask a favor. Now, I know this isn't a conventional way to start a book, and I know I run the risk of sounding like a teacher, but that's okay because that's exactly what I am!

What I'd like to ask you to do is to flip back and read the preface, if you skipped it like I usually do when I start to read a new book. I felt passionate when I wrote it, and it sets the stage for everything that is to come in this book. For those of you who did read it, you get an A for the day and my sincere thanks. I hope you enjoyed reading it as much as I enjoyed writing it.

RG

INTRODUCTION

I am excited to be associated with this book as the editor for two reasons. First, as Forest Gump might say, Randy Gaschler has been my great-good friend for nearly 25 years. I've watched his children grow up and start families of their own. Over the years I've also watched Randy grow as a person, a teacher and as one of the top professional educators in America. I am delighted to be a part of helping to make this book a reality.

The second reason is the quality of the blueprint for change revealed in these pages. Parent-Driven Schools contains some of the most enlightening and empowering ideas I've encountered in a long time. After all, what could be more important than the future of our children?

Over the past year, Randy and I have spent hundreds of hours talking about educational philosophies and discussing the practical applications that he proposes for healing our ailing schools. One thing that struck us as we talked was that we agreed on nearly every issue and opinion stated in this book! This was amazing given the fact that Randy is a politically conservative while I am a lifelong 'blue-dog Democrat'. My parents were teachers and strong union members. On many other political issues, Randy and I stand far apart in our views. But, when it came to education and the welfare of our children, the ideological gulf between us suddenly disappeared.

What we found is that when people are truly concerned with fixing our education system, traditional political views don't matter. The issue simply transcends politics. Liberal, conservative and other political labels don't mean much when it comes to the welfare of our children.

Randy and I first met playing hoops against each other and I was amazed that such a big fellow could be so agile. Later I found that Randy possesses a profound mental agility as well. I am fascinated and left hopeful by the ideas he puts forth in this book. I think you will be, too. Of the many books I've written or edited, none are more important nor their ideas more exciting than Parent-driven Schools.

Inside you'll find the story of a passionate and angry, but ultimately optimistic father and teacher. Randy is a straight-shooter. He doesn't pull any punches here. If you are one of the tens of millions of Americans who are fed up and frustrated with what is happening in our schools, then this book is for you. If you are like me, you'll come away with a sense of hope that there is a solution to the problem of education in America. All we parents have to do is make it happen.

Michael Bowker, Editor
Santa Barbara, Ca.

1

THE COMING STORM

What follows in this book is my story and hopefully part of your story, too, if you are concerned about fixing our defective education system. Since 1993, the year I founded Horizon Instructional Systems, one of the first charter schools in California, I've been called a radical, a troublemaker, and much worse things in some circles. Over the years, we have battled budget cuts, hostile teachers' unions, school districts, lobbyists, state legislators and bureaucrats, and the normal wear and tear of human relationships—all in the effort to give parents a true voice in the education of their children. In our system, parents work with teachers to develop the individualized learning plan that is best for each student. In all phases, our parents have the most important voice in determining what is best for their own child. When I started, this concept was the vision that drove me. I was excited and motivated by it because I felt then, and I feel even more strongly now, that it is the key to resurrecting the failing American education system.

What those of us who started on this pathway ten years ago didn't know, however, was that this simple, logical idea—giving control of our schools back to the parents—would be viewed as a major threat by those in the public education sector. We had no way of knowing that to those deep in the bowels of the entrenched state education bureaucracy, we were about to become public enemy number one.

What follows in the first three chapters is a description of the battles we fought to gain a foothold in this system so we could begin to change it. My hope is that these struggles will illustrate for you what we are still up against in trying to reform and resurrect education in this country. The rest of the book contains my beliefs, philosophies and real world experiences that have lead to my optimism and faith in our ability to change education. It also contains a blueprint for making that happen.

Our Fight to Survive

My fascination with education began long ago, but my fight to make schools once again accountable to parents began in the early part of 1995, in a ramshackle little portable trailer in a sleepy, eastern suburb of California's capitol city of Sacramento. It was March, the most susceptible time of year for raucous weather in the great Sacramento Valley in northern California, and a storm was building. On the morning news, the well-coiffed television meteorologist predicted that by late afternoon a wild rush of thundershowers would swing in quickly from the Pacific Ocean bringing slanting rain, hail, thunder and lightening.

As I sat in my tiny office and looked out at the black and purple clouds roiling up to the west, somehow, deep down, I knew this wasn't going to be just any storm. I had a sense that this one would break with such force and chaos that after it moved on, nothing would be quite the same. However, it wasn't the weather outside that I was thinking about. It was a different type of storm that worried me. This was the man-made kind, and it was bearing down on our old dilapidated office that we proudly called the headquarters of Horizon, our newly formed charter school. It was a tempest conjured up by the most malicious of all sleight-of-hand experts in Sacramento or any other capitol city across the nation— frightened and angry bureaucrats. They had huffed and puffed and now were bent on blowing our house down. The shock waves were coming, and I knew they were headed right at me. None of us had any way of knowing, though, just how powerful this storm would become. We also didn't know that it would change course and roar straight back to the white dome of the State Capitol Building and ultimately transform the California education system. All I knew then was the dream I had built over the past two years was in deep trouble.

That afternoon, with fresh, powerful gusts rattling our flimsy windows and blowing the healthy weed crop around in our parking lot, the trouble came with a phone call. Like all the other office furniture we had, the phones at Horizon had been resurrected from a storage heap of the Western Placer Unified School District. The district had originally granted our charter and now oversaw our new school, which was one of the first charter schools created in California. I was the founder and director of Horizon, which meant also that I was the chief salvager of office furniture and supplies. At least our phones worked, but mine gave off a funny little bleat whenever someone called. It was bleating now.

"Hello," I answered.

"Randy, Bob Noyes," a recognizable voice said. "Hey buddy, I've got some bad news."

It was somehow fitting that Noyes had been chosen to be the messenger of this bad news. He was a high school principal in the district. Noyes had been my boss a few years before when I was in charge of the independent study program for the district. He was the only administrator who had survived the tumultuous battles inside the district bureaucracy for more than a few years. He had survived because he was the perfect company man; amiable, ever-smiling and flexible, he could fit in anywhere and work with anybody. People liked Bob Noyes, even when he delivered bad news. Everyone knew he was only the messenger. He was there because others, "higher ups", did not like to do their own dirty work. They didn't like to face the people they skewered. That way they escaped all accountability. It was the way of the bureaucracy. It was the way our education system worked in California.

"Randy," Noyes said in a flat voice, "the district board voted to revoke your charter. They are going to close you down."

He said it just like that, in a simple, passionless manner as if he were telling me the windows in my car were down and the rain was flying in. Just like that. With those words, he blew a jagged hole in what had become the biggest dream of my life. I had never seen my fledgling little charter school as it may have appeared to others; an experiment carried out in a few old trailers stocked with foraged furniture and staffed by a handful of fellow dreamers. I always saw it for what it could be; a viable alternative to a governmental public education system that was failing to properly serve many of the parents and students in the state of California. At least now I knew that others in the great educational bureaucracy saw it that way, too. Why else would they bother shutting me down? But, that was little consolation at the time.

"Sorry to be the bearer of bad news," Noyes said in sympathetic tones.

I placed the phone back in its chipped cradle and sat for a long time just staring out the window. The storm was on us now in full force and the rain hammered on the roof. On the far side of the parking lot, the leafy branches of a young willow tree whipped around like crazy, much like my thoughts at the moment. I was my family's sole provider with four children at home and another one in college, and suddenly I was out of a job. In truth, though, that wasn't what caused the intense pain I was feeling inside. I was a survivor and I would find another job. What really frustrated me was that a few frightened and powerful people, who hid deep inside the bureaucracy of the California Department of Education, could make decisions that would destroy a movement that was critically important to the future of California and our country. As I sat there the hurt inside slowly began to turn to anger.

Who did they think they were? The more I thought about it, the more convinced I was that what they were doing was morally, ethically and perhaps even legally wrong. I grew more and more incensed that they thought they could get away with something like this—something that had nothing to do with the welfare of the children we were serving. To me, it was an appalling example of the forces that have shaped our education system for too long. I made up my mind then and there that I wasn't going away quietly. That moment marked the beginning of my fight to change the face of education in California.

A Dream in the Making

From the day I founded Horizon Instructional Systems in 1993, it was like a newborn child to me. I put in fourteen hours a day for the next two years, nurturing it, worrying about it and getting it ready for the real world.

I knew that many parents across the country—rich and poor alike—had real concerns that their children weren't being served by public schools. To give you an idea of how the education bureaucracy has grown out of control, government schools in the United States have forged a higher ratio of non-teaching personnel to teachers than government schools in any other developed country in the world![1] Our system has grown top-heavy with bureaucrats. Surveys were published that showed that nearly half of the parents in the United States didn't believe a high school diploma signifies mastery of even basic literary skills.[2]

I was hearing from hundreds of parents who agreed with the assessment that our nation's schools have drifted away from what should be their primary purpose—to prepare our children to become productive members of society. I have always felt that the first goal of public education should be simple and straightforward. Children should be given the tools to become lifelong learners so they can gain and hold productive jobs, while making sound and wise decisions on issues that face their families, communities and the democracy as a whole. Those who are not given these essential tools often make poor decisions, end up on drugs or incarcerated, have difficulty keeping a job, and experience a lifetime of unnecessary struggles. Clearly, they are not on the production side of the ledger. Rather, they drain off society's resources. But, those children who we can encourage to become lifelong learners will remain productive and able to earn a living and adapt themselves even as society and the economic structure of our nation change. That may sound simplistic—that the goal of education should be to prepare students to hold decent jobs—but it goes without saying that emotional prosperity is often linked directly to financial prosperity. Money may not indeed be able to buy happiness, but being unprepared for the workplace and constantly facing economic crisis after economic crisis is a sure-fire recipe for unhappiness. At the same time, a nation of unprepared and undereducated workers will soon become a second-rate economic power, to the detriment of all of us.

They Say Parents Don't Matter

In talking to the parents who came to Horizon, I became convinced that the overwhelming majority believed the same way I did.

Above all, the parents wanted schools to help prepare their children to get good jobs and become productive members of the community. Some wanted their children to become doctors; others saw their children being successful and happy as carpenters or plumbers. As far as I am concerned, the answer to the question, "What do you do for a living?" doesn't matter. That is up to each individual and each family. What matters is that all children—and that inclusionary word "all" is a critical cog in the ideas presented in this book—be encouraged through customized, individualized learning programs, to gain the skills they'll need to be successful.

Most of us agree that the quality of education available to our children is one of the most important aspects of our community. We discuss it in private conversations and education is usually an issue in presidential and gubernatorial campaigns. As a nation, we spend more money on education—more than $700 billion annually—than any other aspect of government except social welfare programs. Some 47 million children in the United States spend half their waking hours during the school year in public classrooms. Obviously, public education is vitally important.

Yet, given that fact, how many parents play an active role in their own children's education? Sadly, the answer is startlingly few. I don't blame the parents for this. For years, I was one of those parents who didn't feel I could play an active role. The teachers and administrators at my children's schools made me feel like an unwanted outsider. I didn't feel that my opinions, comments and questions were welcome at my children's schools. Many of you may feel the same way right now. It is a result of the fact that for far too long we parents have been sold a bill of goods by the bureaucrats, teachers, and administrators who now control our schools systems.

They tell us we don't matter.

They tell us we don't have a constructive role to play within the public schools.

They tell us in no uncertain terms that they are the experts, we are not.

They often act as though we are in the way.

They marginalize us, to use the current buzz word.

They make it abundantly clear that they are in control of the schools and the children—not the parents. Definitely *not* the parents.

I did not want Horizon to be like that. My view has always been that if our schools are to meet the fluid demands that workers, entrepreneurs and business owners face in the twenty-first century, they must be wrested from the hands of the educrats and turned over to those who know their children best—the parents.

I started Horizon—and was willing to stick out the fourteen-hour days in the rickety, old, double-wide trailer with bad heat and even worse air conditioning—because I believed there was a great reservoir of energy and optimism built up behind the concept of parent-driven schools. I was excited that Horizon was a charter school because charter schools have fewer state restrictions on the way they operate and therefore I felt we could more easily harness and direct that energy in order to produce the changes we need. The exact form these changes would take I felt should be left up to each charter school and individual community, but the underlying philosophical framework should be the same. It should be based on the following:

➤ Open competition between schools for students.

➤ Parental choice in every phase of the system.

➤ Individualized learning plans for every student.

➤ Accountability to parents, not politicians or bureaucrats.

➤ Breaking free of our unhealthy addiction to standardized testing.

➤ Changing teachers' roles to become mentors and coaches, while providing more teacher autonomy within classrooms.

Although I still feel that change can—and must—come from inside the regular public schools, I was also drawn to the external force for change provided by charter schools. Successful charter schools can act as competitors to regular schools, often drawing away hundreds of students. In the cases where unions and politicians have not stepped in to crush this competition, charter schools have forced regular schools to change in order to compete.

Parents Should Be Served

Rather than treating parents like outsiders, I met with them on an almost daily basis. My concept from the beginning was to build a school that would be directly accountable to the parents of its students.

I was in an ideal position to start the school in the first place because I had been hired the year before to work as the coordinator for the Western Placer Unified School District's independent study program, which served students who learned at home. When State Senator Gary Hart's charter school bill—which authorized the creation of charter schools—passed in California, a few of the parents and I began to explore the possibility of writing a charter to form a new school. Having always been an entrepreneur and risk-taker at heart, I saw right away what we might be able to accomplish if the school was designed correctly.

Word of what we were doing spread like wildfire that first year and before I knew it we had 650 students signed up for the school. There was great enthusiasm built up around our program. We literally went to the parents and said "We are here to serve you; we want your child to succeed." Many of the parents were flabbergasted by this. They had long been shut out of the process in regular schools, which is why most of them were schooling their children at home.

We explained carefully that parental choice didn't mean they would have to make choices that they didn't feel qualified to make, but that all of us: the administration, teachers, parents and students, would work together to determine what was best for the child. All of our teachers were trained to support the parent's decisions and when the parent was unsure or did not want the decision making responsibility, the teacher made the decision.

Controversial Subjects Not Forced on Students

One of the more popular aspects of our program was that we allowed the parents to decide whether or not their children should be taught any of the more controversial subjects that are now being taught to all students in regular schools. These included religious instruction, sex education, the theory of evolution, and the like. Many readers, who may be on the far right or the far left politically, probably just experienced a knee-jerk reaction to this element of our system. The political Far Left, which has increasingly begun to believe that its politically-correct doctrines should be forced on everyone, would like to mandate that subjects like sex education be expanded in schools, even to the point of handing out condoms to middle school students. On the other side of the spectrum, some people would like religious teachings in the classroom and the elimination of any mention of the theory of evolution in schools. My stance has always been that schools should not be the decision-maker in these volatile issues. These types of highly personal decisions should be left up to the parents of each child.

To those who react against this type of parental control, I would ask that you carefully consider that freedom and choice is part of the bedrock of liberty in America. We consider it our right to vote for whom we want, to purchase products according to our personal tastes, and to choose where we want to live and our own profession. Why then shouldn't we, as Americans, have the right to choose the type of education that is best for our children?

At Horizon, if a parent wanted us to teach evolution or sex education, then we taught it. If parents did not want their children exposed to these subjects by the school, then we left teaching them up to the parent. It was our stance that schools should not force any child to be exposed to any subject if the parents of that child did not wish it. This provided maximum choice and control for each parent. In this way, no teacher, administrator, school board or state bureaucracy could force a child to be exposed to any subject without the approval of that child's parents.

I know that for many of you this concept will bring cheers and the feeling that "It is about time that schools got out of that kind of decision-making!" But, for others of you, a dark fear may have formed in the back of your minds. If you put words to that fear, they might be something like this: "While I trust myself, I don't trust many other parents who either don't care about their children or who don't think about the world the way I do." There is a thought in some people's minds that giving parents control of their children's education will somehow lead to pockets of religious zealots brainwashing students with doctrines that are socially backwards and racially or gender offensive. It is what I call the fear of the "Confederate soldier enclave," as though charter schools were somehow going to spawn a new, Confederate nation. I assure you this is an unfounded fear. There are too many regulations already in place in state education codes, backed by federal and state civil rights laws, to allow this to happen.

This fear, which I still encounter from time to time, is also curious to me in that we allow parents to own guns, drive automobiles (which kill some 40,000 people a year), smoke tobacco, and to have personal choice regarding countless other issues that can and do cause great harm to ourselves and others. Yet, some people still resist parental choice in education because they don't think parents can handle the responsibility. Instead, this group would rather the responsibility remain in the hands of nameless, faceless bureaucrats who know nothing about your child! The overwhelming majority of parents not only can handle this responsibility, they have a far greater stake in the success of the educational system than do the bureaucrats.

There are, of course, those parents who do not wish to become involved with their children's education. They may be neglectful, intimidated by the system, hooked on drugs or alcohol, or simply absent from their children's lives. In those cases, schools must take up the slack and make all the decisions regarding the child's education—much as schools do for all children today. It is my belief that over time very few parents will decline the opportunity to take an active role in the education of their own children.

Given the choice of control, the overwhelming number of parents who came to Horizon immediately felt a sense of ownership and responsibility to our program. We told them, "Nobody knows your child like you do." We asked questions about what they felt was the best learning environment for their child and we listened carefully to their answers. The curriculum was developed for each individual child based on teacher evaluations and parental knowledge of the child. Many times the parent had already investigated various curriculums and decided what they would prefer to use. The school would purchase the curriculum as long as it wasn't sectarian, dangerous or racially offensive. Ours was the antithesis of the "one-size-fits-all" attitude of most regular schools.

Hundreds of parents participated in every phase of our operation, adding wisdom and generating energy and tremendous excitement and optimism that the students couldn't help but feel.

Enthusiastic Teachers

Some people scoffed that I'd never find teachers for the new school, since I was planning such a different pay structure than they had ever had before. I proposed to pay my teachers at a rate based on the number of students they served each year. Since part of our charter was to allow parents and students to choose each student's teachers, it meant that the teachers' pay was based on how well they pleased the parents and the students. This was a critical element of the dream I had for our school—to make it directly accountable to our parents.

By the way, there are some who think that doing this will cause teachers to give students higher grades than they deserved in order to please the parents and recruit students. In my eleven years of charter school experience, this has not been issue for two primary reasons. First, the vast majority of our parents understand that what is important is how well their child learns to learn, not what grade they receive. Second, all of our teachers are aware that they would jeopardize their teaching credential if they were to give an unearned grade. It simply has not been a problem.

Truthfully, I wasn't sure how teachers would react, but to my delight, I found I had no problem recruiting highly competent teachers who were willing to work under these economic incentives. Those who responded were confident, highly skilled educators who did not feel threatened by being paid based on their performance. They knew what I was doing—that I was, in effect, handing the school back to the parents—and they were all on board with the idea. From the onset, the teachers were highly motivated to pay close attention to the parents' desires. From the teachers' point of view, it also meant they were free of the constant stress of classroom management. They loved that. They could focus all of their attention on motivation rather than discipline.

The teachers were not at all intimidated by our charter's stipulation that parents had the right to transfer their child to any teacher they preferred. With this simple policy, we were able to achieve instant accountability to the parents by the teachers.

Not a single teacher I've ever worked with has expressed the feeling to me that they felt somehow diminished in this system. On the contrary, I've never been around a more motivated and enthusiastic group of teachers.

At Horizon, our teachers met frequently with each parent to analyze each child's learning process and to help choose the learning materials and supplies that would most help the child become successful. The teachers were partners with parents, working to create individualized learning programs for each child. Parents and teachers shared the same goal: to fully engage children in the learning process and help them become lifelong learners.

The first year was a smashing success and by the fall of 1994 an additional 700 students enrolled in our school! It became one of the fastest-growing schools in the state, if not the nation. I knew then we had struck a positive cord among parents. It was one of the highest points of my life. My dream was coming true, my baby was growing up! Best of all, I was able to serve hundreds of satisfied parents, who were thrilled at watching their children blossom within our system.

What I didn't realize was that even as we were making plans for expansion so we could serve far more children, the education cartel at the California Department of Education and at the headquarters of the local teachers' union were planning Horizon's demise.

2

THE WORLD'S
WORST THIEF

The first attack aimed at us came just as Horizon's popularity began to boom. I doubled our teaching staff in August of 1994 and we were expanding a new program of providing innovate teaching resources to our students. Out of the eleven charter schools in California at the time, five were in our little district. We had created, in tiny Lincoln, a veritable hotbed of education reform. Whereas regular schools spent practically nothing on individual students, we were able to spend a third of the total funding—about $1,000 per student, on a variety of teaching aids, including additional books, CD-ROMs, globes, music lessons, computer hardware and software, and art and science materials for each student. In other words, that money was spent based on how the parent, along with the teacher's approval, wanted it to be spent. What I didn't realize is that this innovative approach gave those who wanted to destroy our efforts the opening they were looking for.

Their first weapon was a wave of nasty rumors. Some of these rumors were spread by state and county bureaucrats and others were from our own district which we thought was on our side.

"Randy, they are saying you are trying to buy off the parents with VCRs, TVs and other stuff," my associates told me in worried tones. It wasn't hard for me to figure out who "they" were. During those stormy months in 1995, two members of the California Department of Education had been loitering around our offices and asking questions about our operation. I had considered their sudden attention a form of recognition. I figured we must be on the educational map, and successfully competing against the regular schools if we warranted such an investigation. Immediately after their visit they began to claim that we were doing all sorts of evil things and were definitely out of compliance.

Before long, the accusations came out in the open during district board meetings. A handful of bureaucrats and administrators began leveling baseless charges. I will not name these people here because, in truth, the obstructionist educational bureaucracy here and across the country is essentially faceless (and in my view, soulless as well).

As time went on, and Horizon continued to grow as fast as we could sign up the students, the attacks grew increasingly ugly and personal. It was clear to all of us that the ideas driving Horizon were frightening the educrats. The ideas, though, were airtight, so because they couldn't attack the ideas, they attacked the person behind them. At one low point, I was accused by the district superintendent, in an open meeting, of having improperly appropriated some office furniture for our 'spacious' offices without the proper approval from his office. It would have been a hilarious charge, except that district administrators held some serious sway over the Western Placer Unified School Board. As a result, the district board had to take the office furniture accusation seriously. The allegation stemmed from the fact that a secretary, appointed by the district to work in our office, had ordered new desks for herself. I was unaware of the purchase until the desks were installed.

Ironically, my desk was a haggard relic I had rescued from the district salvage heap. If I was improperly appropriating office furniture then I was the world's worst thief. It was a ridiculous allegation that had no substance whatsoever, and it was never pursued beyond the initial accusations. However, the allegations were reported in the local newspaper. The entire episode is symbolic of the type of action that has been taken, and still is being taken, throughout the country to stop charter schools.

The irony of this initial skirmish is that I had often been chided by my own staff and even some of the parents for being a stickler about following every rule in the book. I played a number of sports in high school and played on the UCLA football team in the 1970s. Throughout my entire sporting career I prided myself in playing by the rules. In the twelve years I played organized athletics, I never once received an unsportsmanlike penalty. While I might work to change certain rules through established and legal means, I believe that the existing rules and the laws of our country are meant to be followed. I tried to rise above the offensive allegations being leveled against me—telling myself over and over that it was the concept of the charter school they were truly attacking—but, in truth, the accusations took a huge toll on me. I lost sleep and felt embattled at every turn. What a few months before had been one of the highest points of my life, turned into one of the lowest. My health suffered as did my personal relationships with my family and those close to me. If you've ever dealt with a bureaucratic authority, you know what a frustrating struggle it can be. They had the power and the willingness to use any strategy, no matter how low and underhanded, to get what they wanted. While others recognized that I was the administrator of my own school now, and while many of the regular teachers in the district privately expressed to me their admiration for the system I had developed, our superintendent refused to acknowledge what we were doing. He always referred to me as the "lead teacher" of the independent study program, rather than as the administrator of the new charter school. Although this initial attack ultimately fizzled when they decided I hadn't stolen my salvaged desk after all—our opponents were far from finished with Horizon.

"Too Generous" to Students

At UCLA, I gained, albeit almost by default (I'll explain later), a degree in economics. I had always been intrigued with numbers and economic concepts and I enjoy organizing books, balance sheets, and creating budgets. It's my thing, I guess. So is irritating bureaucrats, although more often than not that is not my intention. At Horizon, I was able to put both of these skills to work. I spent hundreds of hours pouring over our books and managing our budget. We were able to maximize the amount of funding we could set aside for each student by creating a system of budget controls using a computer database that I designed. Then we consulted with the students and parents about how they thought we could get the most bang for our buck in terms of educational supplies. They loved the process and the result, and so did I.

I was proud that we were watching every nickel and making sure our students got the most out of every educational dollar. Imagine my surprise when the California Department of Education showed up at our door and told us to cease and desist being so generous to the students.

The CDE bureaucrats said we were illegally 'recruiting' parents. They sternly shook their heads and claimed that this practice—which amounted in our view to excellent money management—was likely to make parents want to put their children into our school instead of another. This was amazing to us. We pointed out that the intention of the legislature in creating the law was to create competition between schools in order to spur improvement! Meanwhile, even as the CDE was criticizing us for these competitive practices, the state superintendent was exhorting all schools to treat the parents like customers. Well, what business thrives if it doesn't recruit customers? To use our students' expression: "Hello?!" Maybe, that is why businesses spend so much money on sales people and advertising. You think?

Our logic didn't penetrate the bureaucratic walls in Sacramento. We spent the first eight months of our second school year trying to negotiate an understanding—or at least a clarification—of what we had a right to do under the charter law. But, every time we thought we had an agreement on something, we would find out later that we 'misunderstood.' As the months went by, they slowly increased the pressure on us. They began to float subtle hints that if we didn't completely give in to whatever they ordered us to do; they were going to make us pay back money that had already been spent in the school. I was furious. I felt they didn't have the legal or moral right to do this—but I knew they had the power. Paying back almost three million dollars would bankrupt the already struggling district.

Out of Options

We negotiated the best we could, offering to back away from spending so much money per student. This, of course, was the height of absurdity. We had fought and scratched to save every penny that was allotted to us so we could pass it on to our students. Now the state was telling us we had done too good a job. We were passing on so much to our students in the form of educational materials, that we were out-pacing all the schools around us.

All winter we had complied with the CDE's increasing demands. Although the clear intent of the charter school law is to encourage innovative new schools that will act as competitive alternatives to regular schools, the CDE was doing everything it could to make certain that didn't happen. They placed more and more restrictions on us. Each restriction made it harder for us to serve our students, but each time we found a way to comply with their demands. I actually think that this made them angry and what we accomplished was never enough. What really upset them was that we had five-student classes, we put computers in nearly every student's home, and we were spending $1,000 for each student on learning materials and other resources. This far outstripped anything that regular schools were doing. We were out-competing them and the CDE knew it. The educrats were aghast. Maybe charter schools were created to compete with regular schools, but we weren't supposed to win! The audacity! Rather than studying our program to see how we did it and passing that knowledge on to other schools, the Department of Education simply wanted to close us down.

After that it became an exercise in the Theater of the Absurd. We were put in a position of actually offering to spend far less per student. That didn't appease the State. The bureaucrats didn't feel it was enough. We then agreed to lend our computers, software, telescopes, calculators, etc., to students in the other schools in the district. That was still not enough. We agreed to pay for field trips for district students and sponsor special classes that Horizon offered that the district did not. Nope. Still not enough. Rather than share these things, the CDE made us cancel all field trips and Small Group Instruction classes. Finally, we were out of options.

As it turned out, none of it mattered anyway. All of the machinations and ridiculous hoops the CDE made us jump through were just a smokescreen. It was then that I gained an entirely new respect for the state's vast ability to ignore common sense. I came to understand that few creatures on earth can match the cunning of a bureaucrat placed in charge of interpreting a new law.

What the Department of Education decreed was something that came to be known as the "pencil for pencil" rule. In a nutshell, it meant that anything—from computers to special classes—that we at Horizon had offered our students, the district had to offer its public schools as well. What was more; these rules were made retroactive to the preceding year! That was really the key to the entire strategy. This parity-of-value concept was installed to do just one thing—threaten the district with bankruptcy. There was no way the district could pay the estimated $3 million required to make up the difference of the past year.

Troublemakers Like Us

The Western Placer school district, frightened and desperate, was then offered a deal by the CDE. If the district would revoke our charter, the CDE would forgive the $3 million "debt" and call it even. The district would survive and the teachers' union and the CDE would be rid of us. No more radical ideas, no more trouble-makers, no more competition. Everybody goes home happy—with the possible exception of the 1,200 students enrolled in our school and their parents, and the hundreds of thousands of parents of future charter school children.

On March 11, 1995, the district revoked our charter. The following day I received the fateful phone call from Bob Noyes telling me I was out of a job, my school was to be shut down, and my hope, and my parents' hope, locked outside in the cold. We were given two weeks to close the school. Two weeks to collect all of the computers, textbooks, science supplies, tapes, workbooks, software, and materials we had supplied to more than 1,200 students. Two weeks to notify our parents that they would have to find a new school for their children. Two weeks before the lights went out on our dream for a better way of education for these children.

3

WHY
POLITICS MATTER:
700 ANGRY PARENTS
GET INVOLVED!

In the spring of 1995, I knew nothing about politics, and I didn't care about politics. I thought politics was something someone else did. Or, more accurately, I felt it was something that was done *to* us. I had no idea who my state representatives were and I rarely voted in elections. When I did vote, I didn't vote along party lines. I chose the candidate who appealed to me at the time. In college, I voted for George McGovern. During the rare times that I voted after that, I often voted for Republicans. To say I was an uninformed voter was an understatement. Like most Americans I thought it was uncool and useless to care or participate in politics. Because I did not take the time to inform myself on the issues and take part in the political process, my government was indeed something that was being done *to* me. I excused my lack of participation in this most American of all processes by saying I was preoccupied with raising my family and working to keep a roof over our heads. I thought politics didn't matter. I thought it was someone else's responsibility. In truth, I was also a little intimidated by the whole process of making laws, which seemed mysterious and somehow threatening. All that changed dramatically for me in the spring of 1995.

The Lowest Point in My Life

In the normal course of life, two weeks is not a significant amount of time. In fact, if you are like me, weeks and even months seem to race by all the time with incredible speed, and I often find myself wondering where all that time has gone. However, the two weeks between February 26th and March 12th of 1995 remain one of the longest periods of my life. During that time, my wife of eighteen years moved out of our home. There is no doubt in my mind that the fourteen-hour days I had worked while trying to launch Horizon played a major role in our breakup.

At the same time, the Western Placer Unified School District was trying to destroy the most important thing in my life behind God and my family—my school. When the district revoked our charter in late February, we were given until March 14 to shut down and dismantle the school.

Those two weeks, without question, marked the lowest point of my life. I was bitterly disappointed at the breakup of my marriage. Not an hour went by that I didn't try to figure out a way to make my family whole again. I was not, to my great disappointment, able to do that. At the same time, I was faced with closure of a school that represented the hopes and dreams of hundreds of parents, many of whom had become my friends.

"The bureaucrats hated and feared your school from the start," Eric Premack told me later. Premack, one of the nation's leading experts on charter laws and charter schools, was working closely with the state Legislature at the time as a member of CANEC, the California Network of Educational Charters, an association of charter schools. "They disliked and distrusted the fact that you were providing an alternative. Their life becomes much more complex when things don't fit into their command-and-control boxes and they lose control. They wanted that control back. You were a threat and they were bent on getting rid of that threat."

I didn't feel like a threat. All I wanted to do from the beginning was to provide students with a chance to learn in the way that was best for them. At the time, I didn't understand, and thus underestimated, how far some people would go to eliminate us.

It was during this time that Delaine Easton, then California Superintendent of Public Instruction, the top education official in the State, made the infamous comment that clearly etched the state's position and attitude toward competition to regular schools. She reportedly said that while charter schools have a role, the state wanted to make sure there weren't "Hittites working out of Volkswagens" teaching children. Audiences were also told the state feared people coming together in charter schools to "create a school of witchcraft."

It was stunning to me that a top education official, supposedly in charge of our children's welfare, could say these things. It was the epitome of the knee-jerk, "Confederate soldier enclave" fear that I talked about in Chapter One, and I felt Easton was exploiting it to the maximum. But, Easton's statements did one thing. They publicly established how far the opposition was willing to go to stop competition that might shake the established order.

Something out of a Horror Film

The driving force behind Easton and the CDE, of course, was primarily the California Teachers' Association and to some extent the National Education Association. The CTA, especially, hated what Horizon had dared do in terms of changing how teachers were paid. You can imagine the reaction of those inside the teachers' union when they first understood that I was doing away with tenure and tying my teachers' salaries directly to their individual performances. To the rest of us this might sound like a terrific idea, bringing teachers in line with the same performance-reward equation that the rest of us work under. But to the teachers' union it was like something out of a horror film. I was *The Monster* who wanted to prove that teachers' roles should be changed. I was also challenging tenure and the notion that you have to have certificated teachers in order for children to learn. The unions pushed the legislators, who pushed the CDE, who pushed the Western Placer school district, who had little choice but to destroy Horizon. I couldn't help but wonder just where the welfare of the students fit into their grand scheme.

Personally, I was hurt by the district's actions. All I had attempted to do was provide something of value for children. I wasn't making any money and the hours I was putting in to make the school operate smoothly demanded a terrible personal price. I knew the pressure was coming from the CDE, but the district had made it personal. The new district superintendent—Larry Achetel, had retired by this time—was desperate to comply with the CDE in order to keep his own district afloat. I was accused of 'insubordination'. The superintendent liked that word because he was a retired military man. He leveled the charge after I refused his order to stop talking to my teachers and parents about what was happening to our charter school. I was upset at the charge. The last time I looked the red, white and blue flag still waved in front of our school, which to me, meant that I had the right to free speech and was free to discuss with my teachers and parents any issue that I wished!

To some, this might seem a private squabble, little more than a personality conflict that has no relevancy to the overall issue of choice in education. But, these personal attacks, spawned by overbearing pressure placed on the district by the CDE, illustrate why parental control and choice is so hard to come by in public education. The educrats hated our parent-driven system that had so quickly become popular. These personal attacks showed they would stop at nothing to put an end to it.

The insubordination charge ultimately came to nothing, but I will admit now that their willingness to make the issue personal hurt me for a time. I eventually got past it, but you never quite forget something like that.

What was also especially hypocritical, in my view, was that even as some of the administration was publicly accusing us of trying to financially harm the district, we were paying the district 15 percent of our revenue! That amounted to $600,000 per year. This was the same district that just a few years before had suffered severe financial difficulties and had eliminated many of its programs in order to balance its budget. Teachers were laid off back then, and elective classes were drastically reduced. Now, with the money it was receiving from our school, the district was able to hire several new teachers and reinstate many of those lost classes and programs. This benefit Horizon was providing the district was never mentioned, let alone acknowledged.

Rising from the Ashes

I never would have survived this time if it hadn't been for the incredible spirit and courage of the parents of our students. I hadn't told anyone about the difficulties in my personal life, but the love and concern I felt from these parents somehow made my personal pain more bearable. I knew the parents would be disappointed to hear that the school had been closed down, but I was genuinely surprised at how outraged they were. Hundreds of parents were angry and vocal. They had finally found a school that really cared about serving the needs of their children and continually consulted them on how best to do this and now it was being taken away from them. They were being told that a school couldn't survive by putting parents and students first. The partnering of the parents' love and knowledge of their children with a teacher's enthusiastically applied talent just wasn't what the state wanted. In the CDE's view, parents shouldn't even be allowed to participate in the decision-making process.

Then, something amazing began to happen. My ancient phone began to ring and it did not stop ringing for two weeks. The parents began to flood us with letters, e-mails and faxes. People crowded in to see us; they all wanted to talk about what they could do to keep the school open. I was stunned. In retrospect, I probably should have anticipated it. What I was beginning to witness was a natural reaction of parents when they are inspired by a sincerity of purpose, by the effect of their own involvement, by participation in decision making, and when they have witnessed dramatic changes in their children's attitudes and enjoyment of the learning process. I was witnessing what happens when a cub is taken from the lioness, when a wolf pup is taken from the pack. Our parents had seen firsthand what an educational plan made just for their children can do and now it was being yanked away from them. The result was breathtaking.

An astounding tide of energy, created by the parents we had worked with over the past two years, literally swept me along and Horizon, too. They quickly formed ad hoc groups to plan and implement a strategy to get our school back. They contacted lawyers and newspapers. They called radio shows; many people who had never been involved with public issues before talked with great passion on the airwaves, explaining the dilemma. They poured calls into the district board members and state legislators. They talked and planned and plotted and came together in a way that I never would have dreamed possible.

A parent contacted a political activist named Randy Thomasson, who is currently the Executive Director of Campaign for California Families, and Randy immediately began organizing a rally. Randy was amazing. He planned the rally for March 8, at the north steps of the California State Capitol Building. "The Legislature and the Governor are going to hear what we have to say!" said one mom, who had never done anything like this before. I suspect she would have carried her banners to Antarctica if necessary to have her voice heard.

From the conception of our charter school, I had been aware that this new school was important to the parents of my students. Our entire recruitment was by word of mouth and the school had grown enormously fast. I talked to hundreds of parents and they were excited and optimistic about what we could accomplish. I knew how important Horizon was to them. Even so, I was stunned by everything that was happening around me. My small staff and I had been arguing and battling the bureaucrats and educrats and the just-plain-rats who had sought to close us down for months by ourselves. Suddenly, we had hundreds of passionate and angry allies. It was a tremendous relief and boost for all of us. I didn't know what was going to happen, but my attitude definitely changed from near resignation to a resolute defiance. I stopped being worried and I could feel my old competitive nature coming out. We weren't going to let them beat us! Our school was too important to too many people. Maybe I didn't know anything about politics, but I was going in fighting and I'd learn along the way. With 700 parents marching to their front door, our elected officials were going to listen to us.

700 Angry Parents!

We swept into Sacramento on a beautiful, clear March morning, the earlier storms of February having moved on. The Capitol

Building on L Street in Sacramento is a beautiful structure built during the Gold Rush days on the flat river plain a few miles east of the Sacramento River. At the time, it was by far the tallest building around, but now it is nestled among taller office and hotel buildings. Still, the Capitol is an impressive sight, gleaming white and classic in its architecture; with 20-foot high wooden doors, marble statues, and sculpted cupola, all topped by an impressive golden ball. The expansive Capitol Park that surrounds it boasts a beautiful arboretum with impressive, mature trees from around the world.

We gathered on the north steps—700 parents, 700 voices of protest, 700 serious people who wanted the best education possible for their children. We were a noisy, raucous and determined group. One thing was certain—we were going to be heard! Signs were everywhere and people milled around on the grass and on the steps. We filled the entire square. I just looked on in amazement. I had never done anything like this before. I had been to the Capitol on an elementary school field trip, but never before or since. Now I was in a mob! I had also never protested anything in my life. I always thought protests were a waste of time. I didn't think anybody would care. The government wouldn't listen. You can't change government. I thought the way most people think. It's why people don't bother to vote. My dad was a barber and my mom was a cook. Who would have ever listened to them? Who would ever listen to me? In my wildest dreams, I never thought I could ever have an effect on my own government. But that day, looking out at all the noisy, angry, determined parents, I began to wonder.

The energy was electric that day. We were 700 strong and we were without fear. For the first time, these parents had a school where they had the right to determine how their child would be educated. These parents had been touched in a place that mattered to them. Really mattered. These weren't parents from wealthy neighborhoods, nor were they captains of industry or government.

They were hardworking folks who cared about their children. One thing I learned that day is when you give people a role in a decision-making process regarding something that they hold most dear, heaven help the person or institution that tries to take it away. They will fight for that right and fight hard.

Getting Politicians to Listen

My friends who work in politics tell me that politicians react most strongly to three things, financial contributions, media coverage and big crowds. We didn't have much money and there wasn't a lot of media present, but we were a big, noisy crowd. We were all grateful, and I was totally surprised when four or five legislators came out to talk to us. I was non-political at that point and their names didn't mean anything to me. I had no idea who they were. I learned fast after that day, but at the time, I didn't know. I was just shocked that somebody who worked inside that impressive-looking building would come out and address us. They not only talked to us, they offered support. I became more amazed by the minute.

After they spoke, I walked up to the podium. I was too overwhelmed by it all to be very nervous. I had once stood in front of 3,000 people at the Beverly Hills Hotel and mumbled a "thank you" for being named the MVP of the football team at UCLA, but since then I had spent nearly two decades in obscurity in a small town, working hard just to make the monthly bills. I knew I was out of my league here in front of the Capitol Building, with these well-dressed legislators on each side of me, addressing a wildly enthusiastic, banner-waving band of parents who probably would have sacked the place if I had asked them to. I talked for a bit about competition and parent-driven schools and when I was done they shouted and cheered and headed for the doors of the Capitol. More than half of the parents swarmed inside and marched up and down those hallowed halls, making racket and letting the world know they weren't going to let their children down.

It wasn't until later, when I had time to draw a breath and reflect upon that day that I realized that what we were doing at the Capitol was what we did best, we were educating. We found that most of the legislators had no idea what a charter school was and what we were offering at Horizon. They also had no idea what the California Department of Education was doing. It was then that I realized how powerful bureaucracies really are. While the state legislatures, and on the national scale, Congress, may make our laws, it is actually the various government bureaucracies which interpret and implement these laws. Often, there is little or no over-sight by these legislative bodies to ensure that laws are implement-ed in the way they were envisioned when created. Far too often, faceless, nameless bureaucrats have more say over how these laws actually affect us than do our elected officials. Only when the citi-zenry complains is attention drawn to the misapplication of the law.

Well, on that day, we complained long and loudly. That day no one spoke for the CDE. No attempt to justify their actions was made. But, that is par for the course because bullying bureaucrats do not like the light of day; they do not operate well there. They wait in the shadows until the attention has died away, then they go back to work.

But, then and there, on that sunny afternoon, I saw that grass-roots political activism can work. It was one of the greatest and most instructive days in my life. That evening, after our band of renegades had dispersed and we had all gone back home, I remem-ber thinking that everything was seemingly back to its normal state. In truth, things would never be quite the same again. We had learned that we could make a difference, and that reality gave us a sense of hope. We knew now what power we had when we joined together. The following day, our local state representative, Tim

Leslie, swung in on our side and began the process of negotiating with the CDE. By the end of the week, we received a call that an agreement had been reached: Horizon could stay open until the end of the school year, which meant a few months' reprieve. It bought us time. And I already knew what we could do with a little time.

Something Slippery and Sneaky

We still had a fight on our hands. The CDE and the state Department of Finance (DOF) agreed to let us to stay open and not bankrupt the district by requiring it to pay under the provisions of the absurd "pencil for pencil" rule. They also agreed to pay us our earned revenue for that school year. That *seemed* to be the deal, anyway, but I had come to expect something slippery and sneaky from the bureaucrats and I wasn't disappointed. They began slowly, as the heat from the rally began to cool, to add conditions to the deal. Four days later, they informed us they would pay for "incurred expenses" only and we had to immediately stop spending money on the students, although we could still pay our teachers. Then came the real zinger. In an arbitrary decision that came out of the blue with no warning, the CDE told us that we had to forfeit nearly a million dollars that we had saved. Each year, public school teachers are given discretionary money for their classrooms. They have to spend it during that school year or the school takes it back. I didn't think that ridiculous rule applied to us. It made much more sense to me that the teachers spend only what they needed to each year to ensure the students were properly served. I didn't see any reason to force them to spend money on meaningless things just so they wouldn't lose the revenue. I told them they could save the extra money and spend it the following year on the students, if they so chose. Most of us thought it was a good idea to save a little extra money to spend on the students for special, more expensive field trips when they reached high school age. As a result, we built up a reserve that we planned to use later on the students. At the same time, during those months when the CDE had been placing all those restrictions on us we had had to cancel a number of programs, and thus, ironically, even more money was accruing in our bank account. In total, we had nearly one million dollars temporarily parked in the bank. The CDE saw the opening and moved in. They declared that since we hadn't used that money, they would seize it. They gave no rationale, they simply confiscated our money. I suspect that they thought Horizon would not survive another year without that money. If they couldn't get us one way, they'd get us another. There was no other rationale. The CDE took the money from us because they could.

That action, above anything else, clearly showed the bureaucracy's true colors. Who lost in that deal? The students, our teachers and Horizon. Who won? The teachers' union and the CDE. Again, it was clear to me that the tail was wagging the dog. Weren't schools and the educational system supposed to put students first?

Still, we had a little time and we were determined to make the most of it. It was time to get even more politically involved. I knew that only the district had the power to keep our school open under the state's charter law. We had to focus on the district's five-member board. Our fate was in their hands.

A Dream on the Line

Based on our best intelligence (I was beginning to feel like a CIA operative), we determined that two of the five district board members were definitely against us. They were on the side of the teachers' unions and would vote to shut us down no matter what we did. We focused our efforts on the other three.

By now I was well aware that the good folks running the teachers' union thought I was the very devil. I was perceived as a major threat to their cozy little system of tenure, where even the worst teacher in the world was safe from termination, or even censure. But my attitude had changed since the rally. Before, shaken by the events in my personal life, I was ready to throw in the towel when the district revoked our charter. A quiet island in the South Seas seemed to be a pretty good choice then. But seeing 700 angry, committed and vocal parents out marching for their children had done something to me. Their overwhelming support gave me renewed resolve. I was ready for battle because I knew with every fiber of my being that we were right. I felt sure that when people saw what we were trying to do we would win.

I found out during this time that the Western Placer school district superintendent had not told the teachers in the district about the fact that Horizon was providing $600,000 a year to the district. If he had, it would have been much more difficult to win them over in his attempt to discredit us. We quickly went about, again, doing what we did best—educating. To my relief, I found that the district board was well aware of our financial contribution to the district. After that, we went to work.

For the next few weeks, we carefully outlined our philosophies and working procedures to the three undecided board members. We spent hours explaining what we were doing and the parents talked to them about how important the school was for their children. We even agreed to scale down some of our programs. In private, I was furious that in order to win over elected officials we had to agree not to provide as much for our students, but those compromises seemed to make them happy. We had to make deals that made the teachers' union happy and more deals to give the district even more power over our school. The entire affair left a sour taste in my mouth, but our alternative was the loss of our school. I negotiated hard, but always with the idea in mind that we had to stay alive.

Finally, the day came in early June, the final board meeting of the year. We needed a majority vote. That meant we had to have convinced all three of the undecided board members to vote for Horizon. None of us were totally sure how the vote would go. The undecided members had not committed publicly to either side.

I felt it was a good sign that the board had waited until after school was out to hold the meeting. Most of the teachers were out of town on vacation and that would minimize the opposition.

My staff sat through the entire meeting. I was too emotionally spent to attend. They told me later that our issue was the last one on the agenda. To make matters more nerve-wracking, the only discussion on our issue came from the two members who opposed us. The other three did not speak. My staff was on edge. How did the three silent board members feel? How would they vote? For 700 parents, a few teachers, and a very small Horizon administrative staff, a dream was on the line. The vote went three-to-two—in our favor.

Shortly after, the district superintendent resigned, as did one of the board members who opposed us. I will tell you one thing. I am no longer uninformed about politics. I no longer want politics to be something than happens *to* me. I know now that we can make a difference! Also, it is clear to me now that politics and educational opportunities are intertwined at the local, state and national levels. I learned that if you want educational choice, if you want the best for your children, you have to get involved at all of these levels. You may not get everything you want, but the alternative is to risk losing everything. The point is, we can change the system—all we have to do is get involved.

4

WE CAN REVOLUTIONIZE EDUCATION!

It's time for a change in America's educational system and it is up to you and me and every other concerned parent in the nation to make that change happen. What we need is not a reform, but a revolution! Most parents and educators believe that the educational system in America is broken and must be fixed. Year after year our schools graduate hundreds of thousands of students who possess no applicable skills for making a living, while spending over $100,000 per student over their school career doing it! Proficiencies of all types are dropping throughout the nation. Harvard economists recently reported a 55 to 73 percent drop in American school productivity since 1970.[3]

A recent *New York Times* headline warned: *"U.S. Losing Superiority in Science and Innovation."* The article, written by *Times* reporter, William Broad, stated: "Foreign advances in basic science now often rival or even exceed America's apparently with little public awareness of the trend or its implication for jobs, industry, national security or vigor of the nation's intellectual and cultural life."[4]

That's scary stuff.

In some areas around the country, this change has already begun. In the spring of 2004, my company, Innovative Education Management, enrolled its 30,000th student in our charter schools. (We've grown since the Horizon days.) We offer a revolutionary choice to the current education system and parents are embracing it by the thousands. We are hardly alone. There are more than 700,000 students enrolled in more than 3,000 charter schools nationwide, and that does not include those children in private and other alternative schools. Charter schools have now been around for thirteen years. I'll talk about them in more depth later, but for those of you not familiar with charter schools, it is critical to know that they are not religious schools and they are not part of the voucher system.

(For the sake of clarity in this book, I refer to traditional public schools as regular schools to differentiate them from charter schools. Because charter schools are publicly funded schools, too, using the term "public schools" could be confusing.)

Charter Schools, such as the one I was fighting to save in 1995, are effective environments for learning, according to a recent RAND report that stated: "On average, charter school students' achievement is comparable to non-charter schools." They also hold out great hope for the future. "Charters Remain Best Hope for Public Education," *The Sacramento Bee* declared in September of 2004, echoing the views of most observers nationwide.

Yet, despite the fact that most people concerned with education across this nation support charter schools, many of us offering educational alternatives must fight every day to survive. The battle I described in the first three chapters was just one of many we've faced in the past decade. I want to share with you some of the other battles we've fought as well because as parents and educators in California and across the country, you are likely to face the same opposition as you seek a better way to educate your children. The following chapters also contain my dreams and beliefs for the future of education in America. Embedded in them is a blueprint for change. Control of our education system must be regained by those who should have had it all along—the parents. And finally, I'll identify the forces that are standing squarely in the way of allowing parental control of our schools, and I'll outline what we, as parents, teachers and educators, can do about it.

Competition Creates Quality

Like many other educators, I believe that only through competition will our education system yield the most critical imperatives of all—parental choice and lifelong learning for students.

I'd like to take a moment here and talk about why competition is so necessary to the continuous improvement of our educational system and how I came to believe so strongly in that concept. First of all, I believe competition is the perfect antidote to an overgrowth of bureaucracy. I think you already know how I feel about bloated bureaucracies: that they are the death of innovation, inspiration and progress. The human spirit withers inside bureaucracies. Left unguarded and unchecked, they inevitably evolve into tyrannical beasts. But, competition to bureaucracies is what sunlight is to mold. Once exposed to competition, obstructionist bureaucracies dry up and blow away. Human ingenuity and hope grow in their stead.

Competition is the bedrock upon which capitalism and democracy are based. Open and fair competition is a sacred ideal, in my book. Given the fate of the former Soviet Union and Eastern Europe, and the constant struggles of China and Cuba, it is a no-brainer to conclude that socialistic and communistic ideals based on non-competition simply do not work.

In elemental terms, competition—and again I'll stress that it must be as open and fair as possible—sharpens our abilities, and pushes us to new levels of achievement, innovation, creativity and production. It opens the way for whoever can invent the better mousetrap. Consumers rule the day. Please the consumer and your business will thrive. Critically important here is the realization that when education is placed in a competitive arena, the end consumers are the parents. Charter schools and other schools that offer alternatives to regular schools understand this and work hard to serve the parents and students. This type of effort automatically makes the education system better by injecting a competitive spirit into what has for too long been a stagnant monopoly that many Americans feel is failing their children.

The origins of my own love of competition are perhaps rooted in my parents' hardscrabble drive for economic survival. My father dropped out of high school and enlisted in the Navy on his seventeenth birthday during World War II. Later, he settled into his career as a barber in Colorado and then California. My mother attended school only through the eighth grade and worked most of her life as a waitress and a short-order cook. Neither of my parents pushed me to make school a top priority. I always got sufficient grades to keep my parents from punishing me, but I was far more interested in using what little free time I did have to play.

As I was growing up, my dad made a little extra money fixing up old houses. From the time I was young, he had me working beside him, digging ditches, painting, hauling debris, and later, doing carpentry and other labor. I never received any pay or allowance for my work, but as my dad would quickly point out, I had a home, food and clothing.

Sometime during middle school, I discovered that if I stayed after school to play sports, my father would let me out of work for the afternoon. I thought I had just found a piece of heaven. I made up my mind then and there to play every sport the school offered. I went from football to basketball to track and would have played badminton if they had offered it.

Over the next few years, my desire to escape the drudgery of painting and hauling and digging and all the other work I had to do for my dad evolved into a deep joy of sports and competition. In high school, I was so excited about sports that I earned the Most Outstanding Player Award in basketball, became the sub-section shot put champion in track, and even won a football scholarship to UCLA.

Perhaps my keenest understanding of competition came during football season during my senior year of high school, when I became locked into a battle for the northern California scoring championship with another player, Bob Bloom, a halfback from Quincy, California. Our little competition, perhaps only important to ourselves and our teams, nevertheless finely honed my concentration. Because of our competition, I became totally focused on becoming the best player I could possibly be. Battling him gave me a purpose and in an intriguing way, set me free to be creative. To win, I knew I had to expand my abilities and do things I had never expected out of myself before. It was an exhilarating feeling, this breaking down of self-imposed barriers. I exceeded my own expectations and those of my coaches and everyone around me. We competed right down to the last game of the season, when he won our spirited battle by a couple of touchdowns. But, to say I lost is to misunderstand the real rewards of competition.

Along the way, I gained the notice of a number of major college coaches, including Coach Tommy Prothro from UCLA. Never in my wildest dreams had I ever thought of playing for a Division I school like UCLA. No one in my family had even attended college before. But, that is what happened and there is no doubt in my mind it happened because of that little football rivalry. A key lesson I took away from that year is that the true value of competition isn't so much in actually winning the gold medal, but rather it is in the tremendous improvement and joy that accompanies being driven to find and express the best that you have to offer. Fair and open competition inevitably brings out the best in the contestants and greatly improves the overall system. That's why competition remains the engine that drives the American economy—the most powerful and successful economy the world has ever known.

Competition: The Engine of Innovation

I grew up admiring the legacy of President John Kennedy, who discovered his own competitive roots playing football with his brothers and friends in the Kennedy backyard. Later, as president, he often talked about his firm belief that competition was at the heart of innovation and progress. Like most other great leaders of our time, he opposed those governments, corporations and institutions that attempted to block competition. Clearly, individuals who oppose it are doing so because they are afraid of the outcome. They have something to protect and are driven by a fear that they will not succeed in open and fair competition. The only way they can succeed is to keep the playing field closed. In doing this, they avoid having to serve their customers—the parents and students. These groups are protecting their own self-interests through monopolies at the expense of society as a whole. They hide their actions by making back-room deals with politicians and by attacking their would-be competitors. None of us should be fooled by what they are doing. Any attempt to block fair and open competition in this country—whether the attempt comes from business cartels, a fearful bureaucracy, or politically-correct groups which fear their members aren't capable of competing—is tearing at the very fabric of America. We must have competition and choices in our education system, if we are to start the engine of innovation that will convert our schools into places where our children enthusiastically embrace their futures as lifelong learners. Competition leads to continuous improvement and choice, and parents must be provided with both when it comes to educating their children.

5

MY JOURNEY TO HORIZON

Is a good education important? Sounds like a silly question, doesn't it? Yet, if we all agree that education is the very foundation of our society and critical to our children's future, why aren't we, as parents, more involved? One of my favorite people in history is Thomas Jefferson. Besides being our third president, he was the visionary behind the Louisiana Purchase, authored much of the Declaration of Independence and the U.S. Constitution, founded the Democratic Party, and was one of the great inventors of his day. Yet, when asked what he most wanted to be remembered for, one of the first things Jefferson mentioned was his founding of the University of Virginia. Jefferson did not believe democracy or freedom would survive without an excellent education system. I wonder what Jefferson would say if he were around today? Is his dream still alive or has it been smothered by those who fear the progress that open competition will surely bring?

As the years have gone by and my playing field has shifted from sports to education, it is my academic career that I most reflect upon. When I was in high school, I was congratulated for keeping a B-plus average, which was good in those days. Today, of course, students can take Advanced Placement classes and receive grades higher than an A. But, given that I was busy athletically and socially and worked for my parents in my "spare" time, my grades were considered better than fair. They were good enough to get me into any university in the country. I say that because looking back at my high school experience, the fact is, I learned very little! I can still remember some French, but little else. My motivation was never to "learn." It never went beyond just wanting to get the grade. I learned to get decent grades by becoming a good "memorizer" of facts and by becoming a good test taker, not because I was excited about learning. Once the test was over, I learned to clear my mind and prepare for the next test. I didn't have to study much; I finished my homework in class or between classes. I attended all my classes, but it wasn't because I was excited about learning, it was because I wanted to play sports. That sort of motivation doesn't produce much learning. But, it does produce good grades.

Being in class was better than hauling debris for my dad, but I was bored much of the time, like so many students are today. Why is that? Why can't we make learning interesting for kids? Is it possible? Must all learning be a punishment? Has our school system become so mired in bureaucracy that it cannot inspire our children to become lifelong learners?

I will explore this concept of lifelong learning with you later on in the book because I think it should be the primary goal of our education system. For now, I'll just say that the problem with many public schools today is that many, if not most; students are motivated not so much by learning, but by the desire to get good grades. Unfortunately, the two aren't always compatible. There are too many ways to get the grade without learning.

Playing in the Redwoods

On the northern tip of the California coast are some of the largest trees in the world. The Redwood National Forest is truly a land of giants. If you've ever been among these monsters of girth and height, you know exactly how I felt playing center for the UCLA football team. I was six feet tall and weighed about 220 pounds. The players on the defensive side of the line on the other teams typically were several inches taller and outweighed me by at least 50 pounds. I spent four years of my life being black and blue, but I enjoyed myself, primarily because I liked the competitive atmosphere of collegiate sports.

I chronicled a bit of what happened to me during my four years at UCLA in the Afterword of this book. For now, I'll just say that the intense learning I had to do on the football field, or face annihilation by the huge defensive guys, taught me an amazing amount regarding the importance of being a lifelong learner. I had to learn three different positions to play on the team in the four years I played, and much of my early understanding about learning, adapting and succeeding comes from the countless hours I spent getting dirty and banging into people. Life in the redwoods wasn't always easy, but it was a tremendously instructive time for me.

How Enjoyable Learning Can Be

After I graduated from college, I accepted a position at Southern Illinois University as the offensive line coach. Shortly afterwards, I ran into Dick Vermeil, who had worked as an assistant coach at UCLA, and who was taking over as head coach. Today, Vermeil is the head coach for the Kansas City Chiefs. He asked me if I wanted to coach for him at UCLA. I was flattered, but I had already given my word to Southern Illinois. But, it was clear to me that I was being offered these coaching jobs because of the way I had adapted and learned all the new positions that I had been asked to play during my career at UCLA. Football is a dynamic game. It is constantly changing, even during a single game. My ability and willingness to learn and adapt quickly was what they wanted. Learning, I realized was at the core of my success.

I enjoyed the competitive atmosphere of the school at Southern Illinois, and after being dirt poor all my life I was making a little money and had a chance to live it up a little. Which I did! I was lucky I didn't get myself killed. After experiencing a spiritual awakening, I felt that I could not remain in that party environment and live the type of life I needed to live. I resigned and returned to northern California. I met a local girl at a Bible study class and married her six months later. She already had a six-year-old daughter and a three-year-old son from a previous marriage, so I had an instant family. It was exactly what I wanted and needed.

My marriage meant, though, that I had to provide an income for more than just myself. I was forced to become creative. Although deep inside I wanted to teach, I didn't not have the necessary credentials, so I tried a variety of other jobs. I built prefabricated homes and tried selling cars at a local dealership. I was not cut out for selling cars, in fact I hated it and quit after only a short time.

From there, I went on to work for a friend making and selling pre-hung doors. During high school, I had never taken any shop classes. Now I was expected to operate table, band, and radial arm saws, joiners, planers, horizontal boring machines, routers, sanders and much more. Although this was all new to me, I found I really enjoyed working with these tools. Because I enjoyed the work, I also found that I didn't mind learning how these tools worked. I poured over the instruction manuals and bought books about how to do carpentry. I didn't realize it then, but I had just taken some more important steps toward being a lifelong learner. Within six months, I felt comfortable enough with my new knowledge and skills to begin the process of building my own house. All this new activity and learning was highly relevant to me. I was engaged with it—I was learning and I loved it. I spent many hours, especially in the evenings, reading these "how-to" books. I was so taken by these new skills that for the next four years, I ran my own business, building custom cabinets. I kept reading and learning as I went. I also had to learn how to operate my own business—a completely new skill for me. I found joy in that, too. It is amazing how enjoyable learning can be, if you are engaged with the subject.

I left my custom cabinet business only because an opportunity arose for me to take ownership of my father-in-law's auto parts store. Of course, I didn't know anything about that, either. But, by then, I was confident that I could learn whatever I needed to know. I dove headlong into written materials about engines, transmissions, starters, radiators, brake systems, and more, until I knew enough to impress the long-time employees whom I had inherited when I bought the business. By then I had come to understand fully the importance—and the power—of being a life-long learner. I felt that there wasn't anything I couldn't do because there wasn't anything I couldn't learn!

In my life, I have worked as a dishwasher, waiter, short-order cook, bartender, bouncer, carpenter, mason, cabinet maker, antique refinisher, musician, recording artist, computer programmer, car salesman, accountant, tail sawyer in a lumber mill, Southern Pacific railroad brakeman, middle and high school teacher, and school administrator. I have sold auto parts, repaired railroad tracks, coached college and semi-pro football, coached high school football, basketball, softball, and volleyball, and stretched canvas for the famous artist, Tom Kincaid! Those are just the jobs and skills I have learned in order to make money. I couldn't help wondering, though, why I had never been inspired to learn like that while I was in school?

Throughout my time in school I was just focused on getting the grade. I had to choose a major at UCLA, of course, but I wasn't really interested in any of the ones being offered. School bored me and I didn't feel as though the classes had relevance to my life. I simply did not enjoy learning things that had no connection to me or my life. I felt I was being force-fed worthless information, which I then had to regurgitate back at test time. What a dumb exercise! My roommate at the time, Randy Tyler, convinced me to try economics. He may as well have chosen history or math or English because I was equally uninterested in all of them. Fine. I'd try economics. It was boring. I was bored—everybody except a few of the top students was bored. I knew how to get the grade, though, and in 1973, I graduated with an economics degree with a B average from UCLA.

It wasn't until years later that I was suddenly motivated to become a lifelong learner in subjects beyond football. I became motivated only when the learning became relevant and important to what I was doing and what I wanted. I was turned on and tuned in, not to playing the academic game, but to really learning! Certainly, part of that was because I was older and had a family to support. Still, I couldn't help feeling that part of the challenge we have to meet while educating our children is to get them engaged and excited about learning. It has to make sense to them and not just be another boring exercise the grown-ups are making them do.

The Wealth of Nations

During this career-changing time of my life, I happened across a book that helped form the foundation of my philosophy of learning and education. The book was *The Wealth of Nations* written by

Adam Smith—the nineteenth-century economist and philosopher. The first thing that struck me was the size of the book. It puts the San Francisco phone book to shame. This is a heavy book, in more ways than one. It is more than 1,200 pages long! Interestingly, this classic on economics was not required reading for me to obtain my B.A. in economics.

Smith writes with the voluminous and sometimes flowery style of the nineteenth-century authors, but I didn't care. I was so excited by the book that I read parts of it several times. This was amazing because I usually avoid books that you have to lift with two hands. I found it more mesmerizing than the latest best seller because Smith is such a dynamic thinker. He wrote with profound insight about the realities of human nature, and how competition effects and shapes our economic structures. The fact that I tackled a book as intimidating as *The Wealth of Nations* and devoured every word of it just shows that we can learn anything if we are motivated to do it.

Like most people, I had heard of Smith's famous concept of the "invisible hand" of capitalism and like most people, I mistakenly believed it meant the competitive forces that drove capitalism forward. As I delved into the book, I found he actually meant something even deeper and more profound. Smith was a keen observer of human behavior and understood that the genius behind capitalism and democracy is they both are based on a basic reality of human nature—that human beings naturally act in their own self-interest. Capitalism and democracy seize on that reality and are so structured that when we do—as we naturally will—act in our own self-interest, we also act to promote the welfare of others. Here is how Smith explains it:

"Every individual necessarily labors to render the annual revenue of society as great as he can. He generally neither intends to promote the public interest nor knows how much he is promoting it...He intends only his own gain, and he is, in this, as in many other cases, led by an invisible hand to promote an end which was not part of his intention. Nor is it always the worse for the society that was no part of it. By pursuing his own interest he frequently promotes that of the society more effectually than when he really intends to promote it."[5]

I warned you he was a bit wordy, but this is really good stuff. To me, Smith's words described an amazing truth. It seemed to me that the dynamic that transforms this truth into action is competition. Competition allows us to seek our "own gain" while the "invisible hand" utilizes our selfish efforts to promote the general good of society. We build a better product because it will increase our own business and profit margins, yet the improved product benefits society as a whole. To that, I would also add that we are motivated to build a better product only when a system of fair and open competition and rewards is in place.

One of the greatest things about learning is that when you suddenly discover a powerful concept so full of energy and common sense, it seems to propel you forward. That is what Adam Smith's concepts—along with the ideas of some other writers and philosophers—did for me.

My Son Gets Labeled

Even as I was getting excited about these ideas, real life was presenting me with a set of new challenges. If you are like me, you have probably learned nearly as much from your children as you did from your parents. The lessons my five children have taught me are too many to count. Much of what I've learned from them has formed the keystones of my philosophy of education. For example, when one of my sons, Randy, was young, he loved to read. He especially loved reading out loud to others. He read everything he could get his hands on; history books, fiction, kids' books, magazines, it didn't matter. He just loved to read. The thing was he just didn't read very fast. In kindergarten none of the children read very fast, but as Randy progressed through the next few years it became more apparent to us that he read very deliberately. His comprehension was excellent so we weren't too concerned. Then, in about third grade, he ran smack into the "one-size-fits-all" reality of how most subjects are taught in regular schools. We received a letter from Randy's teacher along with a report from his scores on the recent standardized test he had taken a few months earlier. The letter encouraged us to read the report and go over the scores with Randy and help him understand that he was not reading at a sufficient speed. I was shocked. I immediately called the teacher and arranged an appointment. She said that she had never had a student quite like Randy. Even though he read slowly he was the first one to volunteer to read out loud to the class. I supposed that was our fault because we had gone to great lengths to encourage him to read to us. I knew that the more he read the faster he would read. I told her that the last thing I would do was tell him something that I instinctively knew would drastically lessen his enthusiasm and enjoyment of reading. I guess I didn't make much of an impression because a few days later I discovered that the teacher's response was simply to place him a special reading group along with other slow readers. He quickly figured out what was going on and from that point forward he not only didn't want to read to others, but he didn't want to read at all! In one week, the events at school had turned him from a child who loved to read and learn, into a defensive, self-doubting child who wanted nothing more to do with books. It was clear to me that there were serious flaws in a system that could do this to my son.

Disenchantment with Regular Schools

It became increasingly obvious to me that students were still being taught the memorization game, much like I had been taught. Moreover, the environment at the public schools wasn't consistent with the values we wished to impart to our children. Placerville is a beautiful Gold Rush town about 40 miles east of Sacramento in the Sierra Nevada foothills, and is generally peaceful and free of much of the hard-core juvenile crime and attitudes of the inner cities. It boasts some of the finer public schools in California. Yet, a growing number of kids were bringing drugs and occasionally even guns and knives to school. Even in middle school some of the kids were experimenting with sex and the language they used would make a sailor take notes. In the classrooms it was bad; in the hallways, much worse. We can thank television and Hollywood for much of that, but of course, that's another story!

My wife and I weren't unrealistic about it. We knew we couldn't completely shelter our children from this sort of negative exposure, but we didn't want to immerse them in it either. We were far from rich, but we decided to sacrifice buying new cars and going on exotic vacations so that we could put our kids in private schools, which we felt offered a better choice. It created a financial hardship for our family, but we felt it was worth it.

I want to make one thing clear. We didn't really care whether the school taught our children religious doctrine. In fact, I preferred that they not do so. I did like the fact that all the teachers and administrators in the school we chose had beliefs similar to ours, but I don't know two families on the planet that have the same, exact beliefs. I'm pointing this out because charter schools often come under fire from people who believe the schools are all about teaching religious doctrine. This is simply a myth. By law, charter schools cannot do this. Religious instruction isn't what charter schools are about—although they can be structured in a way to promote certain values. I think establishing good values is what the majority of parents in America want for their children. I have yet to run into a parent who values gang activity, drug use, pre-teen sex and children boasting a vocabulary consisting solely of "like" "all" and a host of swear words. There are some in our society, however, who scoff at anyone who uses the word "values" or who might talk about behavior guidelines for children. They say that it is "prudish." Well, if that's the case, then call me a prude because without values and without standards, we lose the very glue that keeps our society together.

The Birth of a Dream

After years of running my own businesses, I began to think more and more about what I really wanted to spend my life doing and the answer was clear to me then as it once had been. I wanted to teach. In a move that seemed crazy to a lot of people who have never followed their passions, I sold my business and went back to school. I was 39 years old, but I felt like I was just starting to do what I had always dreamed of doing. Some might say I overdid it, but I was thrilled to be involved with education and I ended up with teaching credentials in social studies, business education, industrial arts, technology, and physical education.

My first job was in Lincoln on the northeast edge of Sacramento. It was an hour's commute for me each way, but I was full of excitement. I was finally following my lifelong ambition. I was asked to coach the high school football team and generally had a very fulfilling year. But, as suddenly as it began, it ended. The following March, letters were sent out to one-third of the 145 teachers in the district. Layoffs, forced by declining enrollment, had begun. I was near the bottom of the seniority list, so I read my letter with disappointment.

~~The last day of school, the principal called me into his office~~ and told me the bad news. He said there was only one opening at the school and that was for a kindergarten teacher. He didn't think that was a good fit for me.

"Too bad you don't have a multiple subject credential," he said.

"But I do have one!" I said. "It's on file with the District Office. They should know that."

My claim checked out and two days later, I was told I was the new independent study teacher for the district. Whatever it took! I was back in business. What I didn't know then was the independent study position was to be my entrée to my first real look at alternative education. I do remember, at the time, being annoyed at the teachers' union for not alerting the district earlier about my multiple-subject credential. The union had done nothing to help protect my job. I resigned from the union that day. It was a waste of time and money as far as I could see. I found out, though, that I still had to pay union dues even though I had resigned! It was just another example of some of the ridiculous self-serving laws passed by the state Legislature bowing to the power of the unions.

In 1993, during my third year as the independent study director, a new law—with potentially unlimited positive impact—passed in California. It would ultimately make a huge difference to tens of thousands of students and parents, and start a new chapter in my life.

Although I was totally unaware of it at the time, SB (Senate Bill) 1448 launched a new era in California education. It was the charter school law that opened the way for teachers, parents and community members to create and run schools operated outside the public school structure. The idea was to allow charter schools to move away from the current rule-based accountability system to a performance-based one. In other words, charter schools in California would no longer be bound by the fourteen volumes of the California Education Code, but rather would be held accountable through student performance and to their individual charters. It was the hope of the California Legislature that this would produce an environment of experimentation and creativity for teachers, students and parents, as well as competition between schools. The charter school concept, as I mentioned before, enjoyed great bipartisan political support nationwide. The Clinton-Gore administration strongly backed the concept, which helped persuade Democrats in California to support the bill, which was sponsored by State Senator, Gary Hart from Santa Monica.

In truth, I was only vaguely aware of the new law when I was asked by the Western Placer Unified School District to become the director of one of the four new charter schools the district had in mind.

To say that I was excited about the challenge would be an understatement. I did my homework on charter schools and was amazed at the possibilities. My first phone call was to Dave Patterson, who worked for the CDE. He sent me all the background he had, including copies of all of the charters that had been approved so far, which weren't many.

When I got the paperwork, I could hardly believe what I was reading. The law was so open-ended that it virtually begged for someone to fashion a school that was completely different. As I read, an idea began to form in my head. Why not write a charter authorizing an non-classroom program that could be accountable to the parents? The more I thought about it, the more I was convinced the idea would work. I spent some time in front of my computer and wrote what turned out to be my first charter. I took it to Achetel, our superintendent at the time, and while he didn't see much value in education that took place outside a traditional class-

room, he did respect it for being innovative. My charter called for
the school to take all of the funding that was earned from students'
daily attendance and spend about a third on instructional materials,
a third on certified teachers and the rest on other costs, including
administration. We tinkered with a few details and Larry agreed to
support it in front of the Board of Trustees. The vote was four to
one in my favor and I had my first school!

At that time, none of us, of course, knew the rocky and con-
tentious course that lay ahead. But, even as the months of the new
school year stretched out, it became increasingly obvious that there
were deep and irreparable differences between my philosophies of
education and those of the district and the CDE. I had one idea—
to create a parent-driven school that focused on helping children
become lifelong learners—and the district had another—to please
the state bureaucracy that controlled their budget. By midway into
the school year, it was clear that we were headed for a showdown.
It didn't seem like it was going to be much of a fight. The district
and the CDE were much bigger and stronger than I was. They had
so much power I felt I was still playing among the redwoods—but
then, I had been there before.

6

BARBARIANS AT THE GATE

It is becoming more obvious every year that product and process innovations are increasingly made not by graduates of our own public schools, but by people outside the United States. Even if you aren't scientifically oriented, it is important not to miss the underlying importance of this trend. Our economy, upon which we all depend, is based in large part on our ability to invent, improve and produce better products and services. It doesn't take a rocket scientist to understand how critical it is that our schools foster and encourage lifelong learning and the desire and ability to innovate.

Let me ask you a question before we launch into the studies and papers and all the other academic "proof" that the decreasing quality of our schools is a key reason why we are beginning to lose our place as the most technologically advanced country in the world. As a parent or an educator working in the ranks, your answer, frankly, is worth far more than all of these professional studies put together. Here's the question: Do you believe that our public schools are doing an excellent job of motivating students to become innovators and lifelong learners?

If you feel that schools can do a much better job preparing our children to compete in a global economy, then you agree with the vast majority of Americans. A Gallup Poll conducted in 2000 revealed that public dissatisfaction with our public schools is widespread. The survey found that only 20 percent of Americans believe the nation's public schools deserve A or B grades when it comes to how well they are educating our children. More than 25 million American adults are functionally illiterate, including about 13 percent of all seventeen-year-olds. Illiteracy among minority youth can reach 40 percent, and even higher in inner cities. Only about one-fifth of the seventeen-year-olds in the country can write a persuasive essay![6]

Business and military leaders constantly complain that they are required to spend tens of millions of dollars educating and training even college graduates before they are productive on the job. The Department of the Navy told the authors of *A Nation at Risk,* a study on America's education system conducted during President Ronald Reagan's administration, that more than 25 percent of recent recruits could not read at the ninth-grade level, the minimum needed simply to understand written safety instructions.[7] That's a frightening statistic.

Why the Army Can't Read

Only 15 percent of college faculty members said their students are adequately prepared in mathematics and quantitative reasoning. And these are the best students in America! That corresponds to American businesses losing between $25 billion and $30 billion a year because of the weak reading and writing skills of their workers.

When you think about it for a moment, it is bewildering why this isn't a front-page story in every newspaper in the land. It is cause for concern that this isn't a chief issue in every presidential campaign and every race for state office. Yet, we expend more media ink on things like Mad Cow Disease or the latest celebrity couple breakup than we do on the fact that our public school system is mediocre at best.

As if these numbers aren't depressing enough, here are some other sobering facts. The U.S. is not *in danger* of losing its lead in educating workers in the dynamic knowledge economy (which includes the e-industries and dot-coms). *It has already lost that lead!*[8] A key reason the United States is slipping badly in the most innovative marketplace of all is the fact that U.S. high school graduates read too poorly to continually upgrade their job skills. This is an appalling thing to admit. Our public schools are graduating students who are not lifelong learners because they can't read very well when they graduate! What kind of system of education is that? Have we totally lost our way? Our children can't keep up in the information age because they can't read? This is outrageous! It is unconscionable that while many of our high school graduates cannot read well enough to be able to improve themselves and their job skills, the teachers' unions and the education bureaucracy are fighting tooth and nail to keep any kind of meaningful change from occurring within our school system.

Another aspect of the decline of our schools, and this one is of tremendous concern to parents, is that schools have not become freer of drugs or violence than they were in the past. Most of us would agree that those dangerous elements are more prevalent than ever. The zero-tolerance rules that so many school districts have adopted have helped to stem the tide a bit, but how many parents would actually say that schools are safer or more drug-and-alcohol-free than they were in the past? I know I would have trouble saying that is true. But, hey, aren't we at least getting better teachers in our schools? Well, according to a U.S. government report,[9] a smaller percentage of teachers held an undergraduate or graduate degree in their main teaching assignment in 1999 than they did in 1990.

And here is one more worrisome piece of information: Many apologists for the public school system try to argue that while the United States educates all its children, many industrialized countries only focus on their top students. That is why, they say, the U.S. appears to be lagging behind in student proficiencies when compared with these other industrialized countries. That's baloney, according to an OEDC report called *Education at a Glance,* published in Paris in 2000. The alarming fact is that the U.S. ranks seventeenth out of the twenty-three developed countries studied in the percentage of high school graduates. Our dropout rate is actually increasing over what it was twelve years ago. Staunch supporters of our government school system can tap-dance around this fact all they want, but the truth is our school system isn't working very well. What worries me the most is there seems to be no sense of urgency or even concern among the education establishment to fix what is wrong.

A Nation Still at Risk

Some of you may remember the report, *A Nation at Risk* that the Reagan Administration published in 1983 regarding the state of the U.S. education system.[10] It set off alarm bells at the time and there were a few quick attempts at reform. But, over the past couple of decades, the unions and educrats have had ample time to dig a deep grave and successfully bury the concerns raised by the report. If you have a moment to dust it off and read it over today, you will see that many of the issues raised in that report have clearly not been addressed. For example, this comes from page one of the report: "We report to the American people that while we can take justifiable pride in what our schools and colleges have historically accomplished and contributed to the United States and the well-being of its people, the educational foundations of our society are presently being eroded by a rising tide of mediocrity that threatens our very future as a Nation and a people."[11] Given what we've just been talking about, the next section from the report is even more chilling in its accuracy.

> "If an unfriendly foreign power had attempted to impose on America the mediocre educational performance that exists today, we might well have viewed it as an act of war. As it stands, we have allowed this to happen to ourselves. We have even squandered the gains in student achievement made in the wake of the Sputnik challenge. Moreover, we have dismantled essential support systems which helped make those gains possible. We have, in effect, been committing an act of unthinking, unilateral educational disarmament."[12]

The message contained in the report, which is echoed strongly by *The New York Times* article and supported by nearly every measuring stick we have for evaluating education today, is clear: We are falling behind in the global economy.[13] Certainly the fact that other countries are developing increasingly sophisticated technological skills is a factor, but that is all the more reason we should expect far more from the preparation our children are receiving in school. The fact is our public school system is faltering and thus our students and workers are falling behind. By not immediately reforming our education system, we are inflicting grave wounds upon our children, our economy, and our future.

For the first time in our history, we are going backwards in our quality of education. Our children are likely to become the first generation whose educational skills do not surpass or even equal those of their parents. It is a dismal and shameful legacy we are leaving.

Regardless of your politics, I think we can all agree with President Reagan when he said: "This public awareness and I hope public action is long overdue...This country was built on American respect for education...Our challenge now is to create a resurgence of that thirst for education that typifies our Nation's history."[14]

Ignoring Our Future Leaders

Before you read any further in this chapter, I'd better warn you that I am about to get really politically incorrect here. I suggest those of you who are allergic to anything that might not be perfectly "PC" skip over this part and go to the next chapter. But, for those of you who, like me, are more concerned with equity, the quality of our schools, and especially with our future, than with what is politically popular or "correct," I invite you to stick with me.

When I first started Horizon in the mid-1990s, one of the first things I did was take the money we received for the school from the state and split it equitably among my students. Every student received the exact same amount of money for books, computers, supplies and other resources. I couldn't think of a fairer way to allocate the funds and resources than that. This is America, right? Everyone should be treated fairly and as equals. It only made sense, then, to allocate resources democratically, and I didn't give it much more thought as we launched into the school year.

That is when I learned that the state of California does not consider all students to be equal. Moving swiftly, the CDE swooped down on us and threatened to close our school. Why? Because we were told we had to spend more money on the children with larger "needs." These included children whose parents had less income and children with learning disabilities and others whom the state considered "less equal" than the rest of the children. In other words, the state was going to force us to treat our students unequally. The ironic thing about this was none of the parents, including those who the state said were "needy," ever asked for an inequitable distribution of resources. The demand came solely from the state.

In the end, we stood our ground and the state backed away from a position they knew from the beginning was untenable. Still, this type of social engineering continues to go on every day in all facets of our government. It is, perhaps, generated from a genuine desire to help those in our society who are perceived to need our help, but it is one of the most disastrous pathways we can possibly follow when it comes to education and our nation's future.

Democracy in Education

Whether we like it or not, there are finite resources allocated to education in this country. Simple mathematics tells us that for every extra dollar we spend on "needy" children, we must take that dollar away from other children. Often, these resources come at the expense of our high-achieving students. The thinking is that these students don't need our help. The "PC" crowd often points to these children as somehow being the product of "privilege" and I've even heard some educators say that these students, therefore, don't deserve our help. This is not only a ludicrous stance; it is disturbing and potentially disastrous in its prejudicial outlook. The fact is, while these high-achieving students will benefit from our help, in the long run, it is *us* who desperately need *their* help! These are the leaders of tomorrow. These are the captains of industry, the innovators, the scientists, the teachers, the political leaders, and the physicians and the researchers upon whom our nation's future rests.

Will we ignore high achievers because of this mythical concept of "privilege"? Will we punish them because they or their families are successful? To do this is to sow the seeds of our own demise. For their success is truly our success. The entitlements, which are so important to the needy in this country, only exist because the innovators and the brilliant students of America have made this the most economically successful country in the world. It is fine for us to share the economic pie, but without our top students, there will be no pie! America cannot afford this type of social deconstruction.

We must not take away from the needy and give it to the brilliant, but we must not do the opposite either. We must spend evenly. While it may be a cliché', the concept that a rising tide lifts all boats is applicable here. We must encourage, honor, understand and support our top students in every way that we can. This should not be done on the basis of race, nationality or economic status, but on their abilities as students and future leaders. Later in the book we'll explore how charter schools, even though they do not spend unevenly between students, are highly favored by parents in economically poor regions.

One Size Doesn't Fit All

Our public school system's inability to customize each child's learning program remains one of its greatest flaws. For the most part, this terrible defect remains unrecognized and unaddressed. The conventional wisdom among the state educational system for years has been that the more homogenized and standardized it can make each classroom, the better. The question I have is "better for whom?" Certainly this is a good system for those students who fit into this "one-size-fits-all" approach to learning. Public school systems are primarily set up on classroom models aimed at teaching the "middle" students. It isn't flexible enough to do much with the students at the top or those who are not yet engaged with the learning process. The students who can memorize facts on a short-term basis, and who learn quickly how to play the grade game, do quite well within this system.

I agree with John Goodlad and Timothy McMannon when they wrote the following in their book, *The Public Purpose of Education and Schooling:*[15]

> "The search for the 'One best system' of schooling is based on the assumptions that students are standardized and that educational treatments can be prescribed and delivered in segmented form; that human behavior can be directed by rules; and that specifying courses, textbooks, testing instruments, and management systems would lead to student learning."

Herbert Walberg and Joseph Bast, authors of the book, *Education and Capitalism,* also make a great point as to why public education would better serve students if its monopoly were broken up, much as we routinely employ trust-busting of private corporations which try to monopolize the marketplace.

> "Asking government schools to operate in a more businesslike fashion while they depend on the "vagaries of politics for a reliable revenue stream" is indeed asking the impossible. The current public school monopoly explains why schools find it so difficult to appease "disparate, competing customer groups." Mr. Vollmer's ice cream company did not suffer because different customers

wanted different flavors of ice cream; indeed, it thrived by catering to those differences. If schooling, like ice cream, were delivered by a competitive education marketplace, schools would specialize in serving children with certain needs, rather than provide one-size-fits-all curricula that satisfy no one. And it is the public school monopoly, not the inherent nature of schooling, that turns conscientious parents into what Mr. Vollmer calls a howling horde."[16]

I have a question for those who believe the current "one-size-fits-all" system is good for all students. How many children do you know who are exactly alike? How many think alike, act alike, or are emotionally and intellectually exactly the same? If your answer is "none," like mine is, then why do we insist on teaching them as if they are?

This isn't a theoretical viewpoint on my part. I've seen students struggle for years in regular schools; students who are bright, eager and talented, but who don't fit into this narrow "learning band." Many of them get turned off to school because of it. Tragically, others begin to doubt their own abilities and over time come to think of themselves as "stupid." I've even seen parents become convinced that their children are "slow" or incapable of learning or keeping up with the other students because of this homogenized approach to education. Undercut by their own parent's lack of confidence in their abilities, these students don't stand a chance. They falter, lose self-respect and lose interest in learning. Others grow angry and defiant and often land in trouble. We look at them as troublemakers, not understanding that they are simply reacting to a system that doesn't include them. I'm not saying that all kids who break the rules are victims of the system, but many are. My point here is that we are losing a lot of potential success stories by casting out all those students who do not fit into our "one-size-fits-all" system. Let me show you what I mean.

A Tale of Two Students

One of my sons, Troy, was in the sixth grade in a regular school when he suddenly began to have trouble with math. I remember one evening I got home from work at about 7 p.m. and Troy was sitting at the kitchen counter with school books piled up around him. He was hard at work, but he didn't look at all happy. My wife mentioned that he had been there since he got home from school, four hours before! I was stunned. How could we subject a child that we loved to what was obviously torture to him?

I told him to close his books and we began to talk. He expressed to me the fact that he didn't "get" what his teacher was trying to teach the class. He was struggling and felt he didn't even have a good enough grasp on what was going on to ask questions. So, he sat quietly in class and fell further and further behind. With tears in his eyes, he said he felt "dumb." Children's self-esteem can be a fragile thing and this math class was pinning him to the mat. I would like to say I had a magical method that fixed his problem, but I didn't. I wasn't a teacher at the time, and knew little about education. He continued to struggle with math throughout his entire school career. This was especially puzzling because his two sisters breezed through their math classes. It became clear to me that not all children, even those from the same family and attending the same schools, learn in the same way or even at the same speed. I will add that today my son is a successful graphic artist and, ironically, he uses math in his work constantly and at a level much higher than his old teachers could have imagined. However, he suffered for years thinking he was "dumb" in math. He has told me that he still feels that way, at times, even though he has proven for years that he is proficient at it. That experience taught me how the "one-size-fits-all" system can skew teachers' opinions of students' abilities, and how, in turn, those opinions can have dramatic, long-term negative effects on the students.

I remembered this episode years later when we worked with a student, Steven, who had failed math in regular schools. Steven's parents, in frustration, placed him in our charter school in the hopes that things would improve for him. The first thing we did was have a conference with him, his parents, a counselor and his teacher. We learned, among other things, that Steven loved fish. He had lots of fish of all types in aquariums around his room and he was fascinated by them. Steven's knowledge of these fish was at a collegiate level. He had sought out this knowledge by himself over the Internet, by reading books and by talking to the people at the Monterey Bay Aquarium and other places. The child was incredibly receptive to information when he was engaged with his passion.

As you might have guessed, we constructed an entire math program around his fish. He learned to calculate volume and mass by questions we asked about the amount of water required in various sizes of aquariums. He learned other math skills by answering questions about how much food was needed to sustain X number of fish for x number of years. There was no end to the calculations we required of him and he was excited to do them because suddenly math was relevant to him. After that, he sailed through his math classes. He regained the self-confidence he had lost in regular schools and is today nearing completion of a master's degree in biology. The point is when we can customize learning to engage the child and make the learning relevant, when we take into careful consideration how the child learns, and when we no longer try to force all children, none of whom think exactly alike, into this absurd "one-size-fits-all" system, we will then, and only then, truly leave no child behind.

Union Opposition to School Choice

Without question, the biggest obstacles to public school reform in America are the teachers' unions. The clout of these unions is immense and nationwide. They are among the most powerful and sophisticated special interest groups in America. They enroll more than three million members whose dues exceed $1 billion annually.

"They employ more political operatives than the Democratic and Republic parties combined," wrote Walberg and Bast. "Their delegations at the 1996 Democratic Convention—405 representatives—were larger than all state delegations except that of California. More than 3,000 National Education Association and American Federation of Teachers staff officials each earn more than $100,000 in salary and benefits." (That was eight years ago and salaries have only gone up since then!)[17]

Those of us who have been involved with charter schools, or any type of alternative school for that matter, have felt the full wrath of this union clout over the past decade. Teachers in America benefit from enormous good will throughout most of our society, and for good reason. Most are hard-working professionals who chafe under the twisting thumb of the state and federal mandates that often keep them from utilizing their full talents to help students become lifelong learners. By and large, Americans think highly of school teachers; most often siding with them when it comes to wage and work disputes. Unfortunately, the unions cash in on this good will, not to mention the hefty financial contributions they make each year to the coffers of state and federal politicians, when they perceive threats to their spoils of war.

As Walberg and Bast point out, "Teachers union leaders have strayed from their original and possibly noble purposes. Once manipulated by politics, they are now the manipulators, exerting inordinate influence over elected officials through campaign contributions, in-kind donations of labor to political campaigns, manipulation of press coverage of school activities, and advertising campaigns directed toward parents, taxpayers and voters.

"Teachers, principals, and school administrators often pursue excellence or community service even if they are not financially rewarded for doing so, but teachers' union leaders often act selfishly to maximize their own status and their incomes and to minimize their effort."[18]

For more than one hundred years, teachers' unions and associations have fought for control by convincing everyone that teachers have knowledge about the education process and specific teaching abilities that no one else has. They have sold us a bill of goods that this subset of special knowledge and abilities warrants not only teacher salaries, but also their sole control of our children's education. Too often, teachers come to see themselves as interpreters of our culture. It is a lofty, exalted position, being an interpreter of the culture. The attitude is that children cannot learn without them. This, as we know, is far from the truth. Children learn constantly while they are by themselves or with peers. Far from being crucial to a child's learning, teachers must be careful not to become an encumbrance to this learning. Yet, it is often these types of teachers who lead the fight against parental participation and choice in schools because they fear a diminishment of their own "center of the universe" roles.

At the same time, teachers complain, with good reason, that the federal and state guidelines are so intrusive they prevent the use of innovative and effective teaching techniques. In the summer of 2004, thirty-two state legislatures passed resolutions asking Congress to ease some of these requirements. Teachers unions have weighed in across the country in support of allowing teachers more leeway in the classrooms by easing state and federal guidelines, including those in President Bush's "No Child Left Behind Program."

"No Child Left Behind focuses on the wrong priorities for our schools by wasting billions of dollars on paperwork, bureaucracy and more standardized testing rather than giving kids what they really need to succeed: smaller class sizes, up-to-date textbooks and materials, and quality teachers," Barbara Kerr, president of the California Teachers Association, told *The Sacramento Bee* in September 2004.

While I agree with Kerr's statements, I also find a great irony there. Even as the teachers unions fight for greater diversity, freedom and choice in education for their teachers, they are doing everything they can to stop diversity, freedom and choice when it comes to competition from charter schools and other education alternatives. It is a hypocritical position for the teachers' unions to take, and it does not serve either the students or the teachers.

One of the reasons I bring up the unions here is they have not just been a cheerleader on the sideline as the state moves incessantly toward curbing any and all competitors to the public school system. The unions, without question, are the engine that drives this agenda. Bureaucrats, for all their resistance to change, will typically bend with whatever political wind is blowing at the moment. Right now, the teachers' unions' clout is blowing like a hurricane!

Another irony in this story is that those of us who started charter schools are much like those pioneers who started unions before WWII. In those days, union organizers were considered rebels who challenged the establishment. Today, charter school operators are considered the rebels by these same unions, who find themselves playing the role of the established power.

Clinton and Parks: "Far Right" Advocates?

Just how down and dirty these unions can get is revealed in Joe Nathan's book, *Charter Schools*. Nathan, who was also a major force in establishing the Minnesota charter law, noted a number of instances where teachers' unions have interceded either to stop charter school laws or to pass laws to clip the wings of existing charter schools so they are unable to compete successfully against regular schools. One of these occurred in Massachusetts, where unions opposed the state's original charter legislation. The unions claimed the charter schools would destroy public education and fought hard to defeat the sponsoring bill. Even after the charter school approval bill was passed into law, it was attacked by the unions which floated other bills to severely limit the number of charter schools. In the end, the unions managed to limit the number statewide to twenty-five charter schools; hardly enough to do what the original legislation was designed to do—create competition for regular schools.

In Michigan, Nathan wrote, unions threw huge amounts of cash at defeating the original charter legislation. A federally funded study of charter legislation noted that "The Michigan Education Association spent 2 million dollars in advertisements against the charter school bill and its chief sponsor, Governor Engler."[19] But, that was just the beginning. The Michigan Education Association then took the gloves off and got down and dirty. It published a report called *Michigan—The Far Right's New Frontier,* aimed at making people believe that charter schools were a devious tool of the "Religious Right" to seize control of the school system. Nathan found that the MEA's pamphlet defined the "Far Right" as "one of a number of terms used to describe individuals/organizations who seek to impose their religious, political and personal beliefs and opinions on others, usually through deceptive practices, personal attacks, political connivery or stealth activities."[20] Later, the pamphlet further defined the "Far Right" as anyone who opposes outcome-based education and supports charter schools. I'm sure it came as a great surprise to President Clinton and Vice President

Gore, both of who vigorously supported charter schools at the time, to find they were part of the "Far Right." Civil rights activist, Rosa Parks, also must surely have been amused to learn she was considered part of those who would commit "political connivery" on behalf of the "Far Right." The only thing I can take from such manipulative efforts is that there is almost no limit to the depths to which the unions will sink to stop charter schools.

Unions in Minnesota, the first state to pass charter school legislation, attacked charter schools as a "costly hoax." Nathan quoted the Minnesota Education Association president as predicting that charters schools "may turn out to be the biggest boondoggle since new Coke." The president must have stayed up all night thinking up that catchy sound bite.

A Fear of Losing Control

In state after state across the nation, teachers' unions have opposed charter schools from the beginning. Millions of dollars have been spent nationwide to stop charter schools, yet public support remains strong. Despite the fact that the public clearly wants to break up the education monopoly in this country, the unions continue to fight every year to amend the charter school laws to reduce the competition and bring charter schools under the control of both the unions and the state education bureaucracies. Each year they launch new attacks. They are relentless and extremely well-funded.

The California Teachers Association, for example, is an avowed opponent of all charter schools. Former California State Senator, Gary Hart, who is a former public school teacher and the author of the first charter school law in California in 1993, wrongly assumed the CTA would support his law. Being a former teacher, he knew these new charter schools would allow teachers far more autonomy and flexibility to use their individual talents in teaching children. He was excited about how new charter schools would create environments where teachers gained freedom and thus could remain enthusiastic and motivated throughout their careers. He felt charter schools would be championed by the teachers unions. He was wrong.

Hart, a Democrat and chairman of the California Senate Education Committee, had great relations with the CTA, but the union came out swinging with both fists against his bill. The union hated the bill, wanted it killed and the concept forgotten. My friend, Eric Premack, who was working with the bill at the time in the California State Capitol, told me that "right off the bat the state education bureaucrats, supported and directed, of course, by the unions, tried to destroy the Hart bill, and upon failing that, tried to destroy its flexibility." Hart himself would later say that what the teachers unions really wanted was veto authority over charter schools. The CTA wanted no schools that departed from the master contract without its permission. The issue that competitive schools might be better for teachers in the long run never came up. "They simply don't want to lose control," says Premack. "That's what their opposition is all about, their tremendous fear of losing control." Even after the Hart bill passed and charter schools were allowed to be formed and they turned out to be wonderfully popular throughout California, the CTA, with its endless supply of money, continued its unremitting assault against them. "Fighting for alternative education in this state is like fighting a land war in Asia," said Premack. "The CTA makes it awfully hard to win in the long run."

Rekindling the Joy of Learning

More than a century ago, Adam Smith wrote that the teaching profession was moving away from serving children toward serving itself. "The discipline of (schools) is in general contrived, not for the benefit of the students, but for the interest, or more properly speaking, for the ease of the masters," Smith wrote in *The Wealth of Nations*. "Its object is, in all cases, to maintain the authority of the master, and whether he neglects or performs his duty, to oblige the students in all cases to behave to him, as if he performed it with the greatest diligence and ability."[21]

Little has changed since Smith wrote this scalding indictment of the teaching profession. My argument isn't so much against the teachers as it is against their unions, although teachers must come to understand that their role is to help children become lifelong learners and not to attempt to be "centers of the universe." It is critical that we force union leaders to focus not on their avaricious desire to control the status quo, but on what changes are best to resurrect our failing schools so we can better serve our children and their parents. They must ask themselves, "Is tenure more important than helping students become lifelong learners?"

Too much is at stake here for this type of hypocrisy to control the day. We need to be able to reach out to every student on an individual basis and prepare customized learning programs for them. Then and only then will all students be given the chance to maximize their ability to become engaged with the learning process.

Beyond the importance of education to individuals and to the strength of our economy, students must also learn how to be active participants in all the vital systems of our society. These include the economic, judicial, democratic, and educational systems that form the foundation of our country. Students must not only learn how to take part in the democratic process, they must also learn the moral reasoning that is essential to a just society that understands what constitutes not only legal behavior—but ethical and moral behavior. By this I don't mean that schools should teach specific "morals" per se, but rather the basic, non-controversial doctrines such as the importance of fairness, respect, honesty and not doing physical harm to others.

This is not a conservative or liberal viewpoint; this is a fact agreed to by philosophers from Plato and Aristotle to John Stuart Mill and Ben Franklin. It is not only the successful operation of our various systems that rests on the foundation formed by the education of our children—our very culture is at stake. In any endeavor, in any discussion, in any formation of law involving the education of our children, we must keep that foremost in our minds.

7

WHAT ARE CHARTER SCHOOLS ANYWAY?

In talking with people around the country, it is clear to me that most Americans are not sure what a charter school is and how it can operate. What I want to do in the next few pages is to explain what charter schools are, where they came from and why they should be considered just the tip of the iceberg when it comes to needed alternatives to regular schools. I also want to take a look at the precursors to educational choice in this country—in other words, provide a short history lesson on how education has evolved—or de-evolved in some cases—in America. I'll do my best to keep it lively and there will be no test at the end of the chapter!

Charter schools, first developed in Minnesota in 1991, are publicly funded, but they are individually designed and operated. The idea that parents should have a lead role in their children's education is at the heart of the charter school movement, which spread to California in 1992. The intent of the charter school law in California, which is similar to that of most of the other states that followed with charter school laws, is to: "provide opportunities for teachers, parents, pupils, and community members to establish and maintain schools that operate independently from the existing school district structure."

Understanding Charter Schools

Because charter schools can vary widely in their appearance, goals, and methods of operation, there isn't an exact definition that fits every school. Here is a general, if brief, description of charter schools in California: A charter school is initiated by a group of parents, teachers, or a collaboration of both, who write a "charter" that spells out the specific goals and operating procedures of the school. The charter petition must include a number of specific elements, which the charter school is then responsible for achieving. Schools that don't live up to their charter can be closed down by the governing school district or by the state. Charter schools can be "start-ups" or they can be conversion schools, meaning they were existing regular schools that decided to convert to charter-school status. There are strict rules guiding both types, including the requirement that at least 50 percent of the teachers in an existing regular school must vote for the conversion before it can occur.

The charter is the preliminary key to a charter school's success. It must be written in a way as to attract parents, students and teachers. After that, it is up to the charter school to ensure that the school lives up to the promises in the charter.

The idea behind charter schools is to provide alternatives to traditional public schools and to provide competition for them. Generally, a student does not have to live in a specific geographic are in order to attend the charter school of choice. For example, any student in California may attend any charter school. This elimination of district boundaries greatly promotes competition. The thought is that as innovation is spawned in the charter schools it will spread to the regular schools and motivate them to develop innovations of their own. At the heart of this concept is that most American ideal—that competition breeds a better product.

I believe that charter schools can provide a vanguard for a movement to take back our schools. By providing competition, charter schools force regular schools to improve and become more expansive and flexible so they can address the needs of *all* children, not just some, as is now the case.

Charter School Accountability

Non-profit organizations can also form charter schools, usually in conjunction with parent groups. Charter schools receive public funds on a per-pupil basis for every child they enroll. Each school then uses the money any way it chooses, although states, including California, are increasingly taking back control over exactly how this money is spent. Expenditures typically include teacher and administrative salaries, books, technology and other resources for the students. Charter schools can hire any qualified teacher and can even extend the school day and year. They can focus on certain academic disciplines, such as foreign languages. For example, one charter school teaches its students entirely in French, while others focus on music, math or science.

Charter schools have much more freedom than regular schools, yet, in many ways, they are far more accountable, especially to parents. If charter schools don't perform to the parents' satisfaction, parents can pull out their children and the school will have to close. In addition, if the schools don't perform as stipulated in their charters, the charter-granting agency, usually the local public school districts, can revoke the charter, effectively closing the school. This is a significant flaw in the system. Charter schools are supposed to provide competitive alternatives to regular school districts, yet it is these same districts that control the charters. This inherent conflict of interest must be eliminated before true competition can flourish.

Unfortunately, one way the state bureaucracies are attempting to hold charter schools accountable is through standardized test scores. This does not work because standardized testing itself is a poor method of measuring a student's achievements. I'll show you why I feel that way in the upcoming chapters, but right now I want to stick with this accountability issue. Rather than relying on standardized test scores states should encourage the charter schools to develop their own measurements of student achievement. This process must be done carefully, with the final document that contains these articulated measurements made fully public to the parents, the districts and even the media. How each school measures its students' achievements should be an important measure of the school itself. This is a great way to encourage competition, which in turn will result in constant improvement among schools. If a school begins to lag behind in its student achievement measurement standards, it is likely to be passed over by parents, who are free to place their children in schools which are more advanced at monitoring the success of each student.

The original law in California allowed and even encouraged charter school developers to also create their own student achievement measurements. This is a critical component in opening the education system to competition and thus continuous improvement. Yet, it is one that is being destroyed by the current addiction to standardized test scores.

Charter schools are strictly accountable to the state if they do not uphold the provisions in their charters regarding how the students will be taught and how much they will learn. They can also go broke if too few parents enroll their children in the school. Thus, charter schools are accountable from top to bottom, from a bureaucratic standpoint and from a competitive, capitalistic standpoint. If they don't please their primary customers—the parents—then the charter schools will not succeed. Charter schools are the most American of all education systems. They are the better mousetrap, even though most Americans still do not know exactly what they are or how they work.

Bipartisan Support for Charter Schools

Many people get charters schools mixed up with other school alternatives, such as school vouchers. It's critical to understand that while both are alternatives to regular schools, charter schools and school vouchers are as different from each other as night and day. Charter schools are not religious in orientation as some mistakenly believe, and they are not privately funded schools. Charter schools are not magnet or parochial schools. They are not the product of the radical right-wing as some have painted them. President Clinton, civil rights activist Parks, who recently petitioned to start a charter school in her community, and the late Paul Wellstone, a liberal congressman from Minnesota, all expressed outspoken support for charter schools. At the same time, charter schools were championed by President Ronald Reagan and are supported rigorously by President George W. Bush, and California Governor Arnold Schwarzenegger. You can't get wider bipartisan support than that!

In 1999, President Clinton addressed the nation on the subject of charter schools:

> "Charter schools are innovative public schools started by
> educators, parents and communities, open to students of
> every background or ability. But, they're freer of red tape
> and top-down management than most of our schools are,
> and in return for greater flexibility, charter schools must

set and meet the highest standards, and stay open only as long as they do. Also, charter schools don't divert tax-payers' dollars from our public school system; instead, they use those dollars to promote excellence and compe-tition within the system and in doing so, they spur all our public schools to improve."

That is high praise indeed. Leaders from all parts of the polit-ical spectrum, united only by a keen interest in preparing our chil-dren for adulthood, understand that charter schools can lead the way to new frontiers of learning.

A "Home-Grown" Alternative

Charter schools have been called "working, fully accountable lab-oratories in school reform." *(Sacramento News and Review, Jan. 18, 2002.)* Today, there are more than 3,000 charter schools in the United States, with more than 40 states passing legislation encour-aging, to varying extents, their existence as alternatives to regular schools. California went from a handful of charter schools in 1993, to 85 charter schools in 1994. The number has grown steadily since then and today there are more than 460 charter schools in the state, with more than 70 charters pending. More than 140,000 children attend charter schools in California, and that number is expected to double in a few years. Yet, even as they come into existence, char-ter schools' ability to really make a difference faces constant ero-sion not only by new legislation sponsored by unions, but by the clever and intentional misinterpretation of charter school laws by the education bureaucrats.

The reason so many state legislatures have moved to approve charter school laws is to provide school choice to parents. Charter schools provide parents, teachers and even administrators the right and the opportunity to create exactly the type of school they believe will best serve children in the community.

Charter schools are likely to be located anywhere, from regular school facilities, to renovated grocery stores or any building big enough to safely house children. They serve all age groups, from K-12. One school may serve only elementary students, others only high school age kids. Some, like ours, serve students who learn at home. The only buildings we require are to house small classes for students and the few administrators we have. The teachers meet with the students regularly to make sure the students are on track and to answer questions. Some charter schools also allow students to learn in their homes a few days out of the week and to attend site-based schools the other days of the week.

In summary, charter schools foster innovation, can provide more individual learning potential for students, embrace parents as a critical component to the education of their children, and can push regular schools into a competitive race to provide a better product. I think most parents would be outraged if they knew how hard the unions are working to dismantle charter school laws throughout the country. Charter schools should not be limited or discouraged; on the contrary, they should be expanded and celebrated because they are part of our hope for a better educational future.

A Brief History of Education in America

Here's a statistic you might want to bring up the next time someone questions whether our regular schools are diminishing in quality. Most historians agree that around 1840, the northern states in America had one of the highest literacy rates the world has ever known—before or since! More than 90 percent of the adults could read and write and subtract and add with great proficiency. That means, in 1840, in those northern states, the literacy rate was almost 20 percent higher than the literacy rate America enjoys today!

Let's take a quick look at why this high level of literacy existed. In the late 1700s, Thomas Jefferson pioneered an education system that was brilliant in its design. Jefferson's system called for most of the schools in the U.S. to be privately managed, but funded by the government. Most of these schools were local and controlled by parents, much like modern-day charter schools. If the teachers didn't please the parents, they were sent packing. Competition drove these teachers to become innovative and it brought out their best qualities. At the same time, parents who lived in the more urban areas usually had a choice of two or three schools to which they could send their children. This combination of parental control and school competition resulted in one of the highest literacy rates the world has ever known.

The French philosopher, Alexis de Tocqueville, was amazed when he visited America in the 1830s. He wrote in his book, *Democracy in America,* "I think there is no other country in the world where, proportionately to population, there are so few ignorant and so many learned individuals as in America."[22]

Unfortunately, this incredible model of learning efficiency disappeared not long afterwards. It faded into mediocrity as the government gained control of the schools, unions gained control of the government and Jefferson's plan went out the window. During the mid-to-late 1800s, schools became homogenized. In one of the colossal mistakes in our country's history, the educational bureaucrats began to transform the nation's schools from the Jeffersonian model to an educational model that was popularized in what was then Prussia. Undoubtedly it was the Prussian model's top-down control of the school system by the government that appealed to these bureaucrats. Prussia at the time wasn't a capitalistic nation, had no history of open and fair competition, and its systems were run by autocrats. Centralized control, standardized teachers' pay, and state-enforced uniformity within each school appealed to those gaining power over America's schools. Where did the question of how best to educate our children fit into all of this? It didn't. It was cumbersome and got in the way of creating a great and shining bureaucracy where mediocre thinkers and cowardly characters could become kings and queens.

It was logical then, as time went on, that the push for standardized learning became the rage. Competition between schools and teachers ceased. In its place, the "one-size-fits-all" attitude toward teaching children grew. As the power over the schools shifted from the parents to the school bureaucracies, innovation diminished and calcifying concepts like tenure began to flourish. The most efficient education system in the world was disassembled to the benefit of a few and the detriment of many.

During the ensuing decades, there were voices calling for school choice. Adam Smith, Thomas Paine, John Stuart Mill, Nobel Prize-winning economist Milton Friedman and many others called out for some type of school choice. Mill dismissed public schools as "A mere contrivance for molding people to be exactly like one another." But even the voices of these brilliant men weren't enough. Or, more accurately, their voices couldn't compete with the power of the bureaucrats and later, the political contributions from the unions.

Friedman's call for alternatives to regular schools in the 1950s and 60s did gain some public notice, but out of his original concepts for school choice came the idea of school vouchers. These became quite controversial and have actually muddied the waters when it comes to charter schools. People get vouchers and charter schools mixed up all the time, and consequently, many Americans feel that charter schools are created, supported and operated by the Religious Right. I can't tell you how many times

I've had to dispel this idea, especially with more politically liberal folks. I tell them that quite the contrary; by law charter schools *cannot* dictate religious doctrine to their students.

Despite the unions' hold on the education system, slowly, in the latter part of the twentieth century, the seeds of discontent began to grow among parents. It was becoming clear to many that our schools, once the sleekest, most efficient learning centers in the world, had become inefficient, lumbering, administratively-heavy bureaucracies where teachers were sometimes reduced to serving as little more than expensive baby sitters.

The First Charter School Law

The first real rumblings for meaningful reform began, as it often does, in the northern Great Lakes states. In this case, it was Minnesota where the first breakthroughs occurred. State Senator Ember Reichgott-Junge first introduced the charter school concept to the Minnesota Senate in 1990. Eric Premack, who had just graduated from the University of Chicago, was involved with this legislation. Eric told me an interesting story of a meeting he had attended just before the Minnesota law was approved.

"I was working to help Senator Reichgott-Junge in 1990 when one of my colleagues dragged me to a high-rise law office in downtown Minneapolis," Eric recalled. "There was etched glass and mahogany all around and I was in awe of the place. Inside the room were some of the top people from business and education from throughout the Minneapolis area. The purpose of the meeting was for the CEOs and managers of these private companies to explain to the educators how they did business in private enterprise. The idea was for the educators to begin to integrate these concepts and practices into their approach to education. It was a real eye-opener for the educators. It led to some of the reforms such as open enrollment. There were many of these types of discussions over the next few years. I think it really helped the educators generate more progressive ideas."

As you might have expected, Senator Reichgott-Junge was immediately attacked by the teachers' unions and her bill was defeated. But, to the unions' dismay, the idea did not die. The concept of competition in schools was too powerful for even the unions to kill. In 1991, the Minnesota Legislature managed something that would have put a smile on Thomas Jefferson's face; they passed the first charter school law in the country. In the long run, I believe the action that Minnesota took will be looked upon as an important milestone in the history of education in this country. Yet, supporters, including Senator Reichgott-Junge weren't sure just how much of a victory it had been.

"I was delighted and disappointed," Reichgott-Junge said.[23] "Delighted that the concept had been accepted. Disappointed that the provisions were so weak."

Her equivocation was due to the fact that while the unions were not able to stop the bill entirely, they had managed to damage it. They were able to push through a cap on the number of charter schools allowed and to place a number of other restrictions on what they saw as a direct threat to their control of the education monopoly. Still, it was a victory for those who championed school choice for parents. Although watered down, the concept that the unions feared most—competition—had become a reality. It was no longer a theory—it had form in Minnesota charter schools. Innovative people around the country who wanted more out of our education system suddenly took notice. One of them was a former school teacher, a state senator in the most populous state in the union—California.

California's Charter Law

Gary Hart holds a bachelor's degree in history from Stanford University and a master's degree in education from Harvard University. He was one of the first people in California to understand how exciting it would be to bring the charter school concept to the Golden State. As the chairman of the State Senate Education Committee from 1983 to 1995, Hart had already authored a number of important education bills that helped middle-income families afford higher education, improved school funding and strengthened academic performance standards throughout the state. To those who still hold to the mistaken belief that charter schools are strictly the creation of political conservatives, it will surprise you to know that Hart was a progressive Democrat, who authored a number of tough anti-pollution bills that included increasing penalties for oil and chemical spills statewide. In 1990, the environmentally-oriented Planning and Conservation League named him the Environmental Legislator of the Year.

In my view, at least, none of Hart's considerable political accomplishments was more important than the legislation he wrote, SB 1448, which created charter schools in California. I believe that California's involvement in the charter school movement was critical to the movement's survival. California, although losing its lead in many ways as the most innovative and daring state in the union, still maintains a high profile. What happens in California is often nationwide news. Once California got in on the act, dozens of other states followed.

Republican Governor Pete Wilson backed the Hart bill and signed it into law. Thus, the first charter school bill in California was written by a champion of the Left, and signed by a conservative governor.

The California Teachers Association opposed the bill from the beginning. The image that comes to mind is a pack of wolves nipping at the heels of a bull elk, circling, snarling and snapping, trying to bring down the much stronger animal. This time, though, the wolves went hungry.

However, the story unfortunately does not stop there. "Right off the bat the bureaucrats within the California Department of Education tried to destroy the flexibility of Hart's bill," said Premack. "In every way that the charter school law allowed for competition and innovation, CDE tried to curb it. There was, and still is, a persistent and on-going attempt in California, by the bureaucracy, to make all charter schools look just like government-run regular schools. You know; the thirty students in a cell with a bell system."

Like the old Sonny and Cher song, *The Beat Goes On,* the fight to keep school choice and charter schools alive in California and across the nation continues every day. It gets wearisome and frustrating at times because most of us who are working with charter schools would much rather be spending our time and energy on creating better learning environments for our students.

8

THE GROWTH YEARS

Perhaps there was no better example of this bureaucratic harassment than what we experienced in 1995. We may have won the battle in Sacramento to keep our school alive, but the war was far from over. I would love to say we all lived happily ever after, but during our fight in the spring of that year, we had lost a lot of ground. We still had a school but it was far from the one I had envisioned. The CDE hadn't been able to force the district to close us down, but they were ratcheting down our spending in an effort to keep us from being an attractive alternative to parents. We had to close all of our special classes and our field trips, and vastly limit the resources we could provide students. We had to amend our charter to appease the teachers' union and we had to give the district more control over our school. We couldn't even provide decent textbooks, let alone a complete individualized learning plan for each child, which was my overall plan and dream. As a result, more than 400 of our students dropped out and went elsewhere. It appeared that the CDE's plan to get rid of us was working. They couldn't beat us in a straight-up competition at the Capitol, so they were making an end-run in the darkness.

Sitting in my small office I wondered if after all that we had been through, we were finally going to have to throw in the towel and give up. Then it occurred to me that this wasn't a fight we were going to win alone. We had allies at the Capitol in Sacramento. They had spoken kindly about our efforts at the rally; maybe it was time to put those words to the test. At the same time, I wondered if we could find a law firm that would help us make a legal case against what CDE was doing. I went to work on both fronts.

Our first step was to request a Legislative Counsel opinion on whether the CDE's interpretation of Senator Hart's bill was consistent with the intent of the law. Assemblyman David Knowles made the request for us, and to our delight, the Legislative Counsel, who reviews legislation and makes legal findings for the California State Legislature; found that the CDE was indeed exceeding its authority in hammering us with financial restrictions. The CDE's response was to shrug it off as just another legal opinion. It gives you an idea of the lofty position in which the CDE held itself. We were encouraged, but knew we had to bring in some heavier hitters. Next, with the assistance from members of California Network of Educational Charters, the organization of charter schools in California, we asked Senator Hart for his opinion as to whether the CDE was interpreting his law in the proper way.

Senator Hart's response to us was explosive. He wrote a letter stating that the CDE was far from complying with the spirit or the letter of the law; rather the CDE's actions were actually contradicting the law. When we got his letter, we were ecstatic. It was perfect! We thought he might react this way, but this was even more than we had hoped for. The CDE was going to have difficulty shrugging off this document as just another opinion!

We didn't stop there. One of the parents knew State Senator, Steve Baldwin, and he filed a request with the California State Attorney General (AG) for an official opinion on the CDE's actions. (I don't want to get bogged down in the minutia of this battle, but it is important, I feel, for those of you involved now with charter schools to know about all the weapons that are available to you when you find yourself skirmishing with the bureaucracy.) Anyway, the AG at the time, Dan Lungren, was a Republican who we felt might support us. Republicans, in general, like the idea of parental rights and local control, although as I've pointed out, charter schools have enjoyed widespread bipartisan support.

It was so political at that point, we fretted over whether Senator Baldwin might actually be too conservative to get the kind of traction necessary to have the attorney general consider the case. Mr. Lungren was known to be a moderate. You would hope this type of political intrigue wouldn't be a part of finding the best ways to teach our children, but reality is reality and there we were. It was either play the game or give up. I wasn't about to give up. A short time later, we breathed a deep sigh of relief when the attorney general agreed to provide us with an opinion. It would take a matter of months before he could get to the case, but if he did ultimately agree with our interpretation of the law, it would mean that in any future legal action we might take against the CDE, they would have to use their own lawyers to defend themselves. They would also know we would have the state's own legal counsel on our side.

While we waited for the attorney general's opinion, we remained busy. I found a large legal firm in Los Angeles, Chadborne and Park, which agreed to take our case against the CDE on a pro bono basis. At the same time, another of my friends from CANEC, Pam Riley, arranged for us to meet with a lawyer from the San Francisco-based Pacific Legal firm, which agreed to represent the Western Placer Unified School District in our fight. The majority of the district board members, headed by Rhynie Hollitz, was supportive of our efforts. It was fantastic that such a prestigious firm would take our case for free because we didn't have any money! One of the ploys the CDE was trying to use

against us was to drain our resources so we wouldn't have money
left to hire legal representation. Clever, but in this case it didn't
work. By now, I realized fully that the stakes were higher than ever
before. I was a long way from dreaming of a better way to educate
children in my little office in Lincoln. Charter school administrators throughout the state and the country were watching because
they knew our fate would be their own. I was still in the land of the
redwoods, but I wasn't intimidated, and I wasn't going to give up.

Cowboy Boots and All

I still suspect that one of the reasons the CDE underestimated us
was my old, scuffed cowboy boots. I wore them everywhere, into
the Capitol, at rallies, at hearings and throughout the hallowed
halls of the bureaucracy. I know it drove the guys in $2,000 suits
and $200 wing-tipped shoes, nuts. They thought I was a hick cow-
boy and I probably was. Premack and Patterson told me later that
the highly-paid Capitol insiders enjoyed making jokes about my
attire. "They stopped laughing, though, when you got the attorney
general's opinion back and it was in your favor and when your
friends from Chadborne and Park and Pacific Legal showed up on
your side," said Patterson. "It made them crazy that you beat them
at their own game."

The combination of the AG's opinion, followed by our threat
of a law suit, forced the CDE back to the table. They were especially surprised that we were ready to go to court. It is rare for a
district or school to sue the state because most administrators are
afraid of future retribution. I was ready to play our hand all the way
through, though, because we had little to lose. Reluctantly, the
CDE drew up a new agreement that specified that we had the right
to go back to doing all the things we were doing before. The agreement was especially important because it applied not only to us,

but to all charter schools in California. The agreement allowed charter schools to place computers in students' homes, to spend as much money as we wanted to on instructional materials, and to offer classes with as low a teacher-student ratio as we chose. These were major victories for charter schools throughout the state. The "pencil for pencil" concept was thrown out the window. This was especially gratifying to me because if we hadn't forced this absurd concept into the light, the CDE would most likely still be enforcing it today. In the end, it was the energy and passion of the parents that made this happen. If it hadn't been for the rally at the Capitol, Horizon's plight would have gone unnoticed. The rally lifted our profile and visibility, and convinced the two legal firms to represent us on a pro bono basis. They rallied around Horizon because I was simply saying what they already believed, that parents should play a major role in determining the quality of education their children received. Perhaps for the first time in its history, the CDE was forced to agree. David had overcome Goliath with the help of hundreds of parents!

In truth, though, while it seemed a great victory at the time, we were simply back where we had been eighteen months before. We had spent all that time and energy simply to get back to square one. The shame in all of this is that we should have been spending this time and energy on educating children, not fighting political battles. What especially annoyed me was that, as usual when bureaucrats bumble or intentionally try to subvert a progressive plan, there was no accountability. No one was ever held responsible for this terrible waste of time, energy and resources.

The $1 Million Heist

In the spring of 1996, shortly after the CDE signed the agreement allowing us to get back to business as usual—which was a tacit admission that Horizon broke no rules and did nothing wrong—we asked for a return of the nearly $1 million that the CDE had withheld from us earlier. The money was critical to our students and we felt we rightly should have had it restored to us. In classic bureaucratic style, though, the CDE immediately shrugged off any responsibility. They told us that the California State Department of Finance had control over the funds and we had to deal with them if we wanted the money. I was frustrated because there is no effective system of oversight for state bureaucracies. They are able to play this kind of bureaucratic shell game without fear of being held accountable. The Department of Finance did not say specifically that we did anything wrong, but they told us that because they hadn't been part of the deal between Horizon and the CDE, they didn't have to pay the money back to us! This was mind-blowing to me. I felt like I had fallen down the rabbit hole and was talking to Twiddledum and the Mad Hatter. It was as if the state could make up any rule they chose and we were totally at their mercy. We never received the money.

Exciting New Advances

Despite the loss of those funds, we were excited to be back in business at the beginning of the new school year in 1996. A part of me was frustrated that we had to spend so much time trying to appease the CDE. Instead of being in our fourth year of development it was almost as if we had been in a time warp for the previous two years. But, I soon left that frustration behind because we charged ahead and began doing everything possible to bring more and better services to our students and parents. We developed our own Internet access for all our students so they could go online without paying for server fees. We created a computer service department to keep up with maintenance and training. We expanded our teacher training department so we could assist our teachers in finding the best learning opportunities available for their students. We set up online classes with new video teleconferencing software. We also set up satellite dish stations that pumped high school classes into our students' homes.

In a short time, word spread and we gained back our old students and then some. Within two years, we were serving more than 2,000 students and more were enrolling every day. The biggest challenge was finding and training teachers to keep up with the demand. We even began developing staff training programs on-line so teachers could learn from their homes at night until their training was completed. That way many of them could keep their regular jobs teaching in traditional schools until they were trained to teach in our programs. This was not an insignificant effort because few of the teachers, even the ones with years of experience, had the knowledge and skills necessary to match the curriculum and different types of learning approaches we offered. We didn't just give lip service to our mission of individualizing each student's learning program. Some members of our training staff did nothing else but evaluate different education programs and textbooks. They then wrote up evaluations that included information about what kind of student could best be served by each.

At the same time, we put everything we had on the Internet so it could be shared with anyone interested in the information. We included all of our forms, documents, school practices and policies, curriculum options, and anything else we thought might be useful to anyone interested in educating children. We offered to provide help to regular schools interested in establishing any of our programs, free of charge.

During this time we were gaining a full six-year accreditation, the maximum possible, from the region's accrediting agency, the Western Association of Schools and Colleges (WASC). It was rare for a first-time accredited school to receive

long-term accreditation status and even more rare for a non-classroom program to get it. What especially impressed the WASC was
the breadth of our offerings to students. We purchased learning
materials from more than 700 vendors and the average time from
teacher request to delivery was less than three weeks. This was in
an industry that typically took several months to get the same
materials. They also expressed approval of the various measures
we had in place to ensure accountability. By this time we had six
different departments managing all of the processes necessary to
provide individual learning programs to all students. Our student
records, attendance, purchasing, shipping and receiving, training
and computer technology departments all aimed at maximum efficiency and accountability. We took great care to ensure that not a
penny was spent that could not be accounted for. We continued to
focus on maximizing student learning. We were able to provide
both the wide variety and accountability by using our computer
databases to track everything. Our mission was to be technologically innovative by automating processes that had never before
been automated in schools, which saved us a great deal of money
in the long run. We were also extremely careful with our spending
procedures. Our goal was to save as much money as possible. This
was contrary to the outlook in most regular schools where teachers
and administrators are encouraged to spend all the money they are
allotted or face having their budgets reduced the following year.

The two years that followed were some of the more satisfying years of my career. We were growing, the idea of school choice
was growing and I was filled with optimism and satisfaction.
Parents continually called or showed up at my office door, expressing their excitement and approval over how our school was serving their children. We were on a mission, a quest to provide the
best future possible for all of our students, and there was nothing
but blue skies ahead. So I thought at the time.

9

KIDS ARE LEARNING MACHINES—UNTIL THEY GET TO SCHOOL!

What do you think Bill Gates would do if his workers suddenly tried to establish the concept of tenure within Microsoft? What if they wanted a provision in the company that stated that no one who had worked there for a certain number of years could ever be fired regardless of the quality of their work? Can you imagine any successful business owner or manager allowing the concept to be introduced into their companies? What do you think would happen to the quality of their products if tenure was a part of company policy? The question then becomes, are products like computer software more important than the future of our children? Then why do we not allow tenure in private companies, but we accept it in our schools?

As you might imagine, this line of thinking does not endear me to the teachers' unions. They hated my system of paying teachers per pupil signed up for their classes. As I've mentioned, parents and students could choose which teachers they wanted, therefore, teachers were at once accountable to the parents under my system.

The education bureaucracy was cut out of the deal. Who are the winners in this deal? The parents, the students and the teachers. Who loses control? The unions and the bureaucracy. It's not hard to guess why we became such a target of these two groups.

New Roles for Teachers.

It is critically important that we redefine the teaching profession in California and America. By the way, most of the good teachers I talk to whole-heartedly support what I am proposing.

During those growing years of the mid-1990s, one of the concepts that I used to help create the framework of Horizon was the idea that learning to learn should not be punishment for a child. Whoever said learning had to be painful? Why do public schools so often force this notion onto the children they service? Why do so many educrats feel that making learning drudgery is in some way a noble enterprise? There are no good answers to these questions. The obvious truth is the more painful we make it for children to learn, the less they will want to learn! The vast majority of students learn far better and faster if they are engaged in the subject and the process. How are you going to help and encourage a child to become a life-long learner if you're teaching him or her that learning is painful? It didn't make sense to me then and it doesn't make sense to me now.

From the beginning, our teachers knew one of their great challenges was to learn what interested each child and how to integrate that passion into the learning process. That, I admit, is a radical concept to most teachers and even many parents. Some instinctively feel that working to understand how an individual child learns is somehow pandering and spoiling the child; and that the child, instead, should have his or her nose put to the "grindstone" and learn whatever and however the instructor chooses to present the material! I always wondered how anyone could think that attitude is supposed to motivate a child to want to continue to learn. I know I never liked the word "grindstone" especially if someone was going to put my nose to it. The fact is, our football practices at UCLA and in high school were grueling and surely qualified as "grindstones," but I didn't see it that way because I loved the game. Because I loved it the hard work didn't seem excruciating at all. If I didn't exactly enjoy some of the tougher workouts, especially early in the season when it was sweltering hot on the practice field, I was nevertheless interested, engaged and excited to do whatever it took to improve. That's why, in the mid-1990s, I felt strongly that if we could get students, especially those who had never shown an interest in academics before, interested, engaged and excited about learning, they would do whatever it took to improve and therefore we would be successful and so would they.

Children are natural learners. If you've ever watched young, pre-school children exploring their world, you know what I mean. At that stage, we generally haven't put their noses to the grindstone yet, and they are learning about their world with great leaps and bounds of enthusiasm. They explore, test, study, absorb, touch, taste, mimic, and watch everything around them. Most researchers will tell you very young children can learn as many languages as they are exposed to. They are proverbial "open books" to the world around them. Their senses are wide open, their minds absorbing knowledge like a sponge. Children at that age are learning machines. Then we parents take them to school and drop them off. All too often, the learning, or at least the excitement for learning, stops within a few years for various reasons. Above all else, I didn't want that to happen to our students. I wanted them to stay excited about learning. That was the challenge I put before our teachers. I wanted them to keep those little learning machines turned on!

The individualized learning plan for each student became the centerpiece for our school and our mission to engage every child.

Before the school year began, I had my teachers meet with each of the students and their parents. We asked questions that led us to an understanding of what each student was interested in and how they learned best. It required a different skill set from our teachers than what had been required of them in public schools. This analytical skill was critical for our teachers; they had to know how to put together an individualized learning program and then how to carry it out. This took time. Most regular school teachers don't even consider this type of approach because it takes more effort and has never been required of them. That's because regular schools do not expect to reach all the students. Regular schools, and unfortunately many parents, have acquiesced to the perceived notion that it is inevitable that a certain portion of our children will fail in regular schools. Frighteningly, many Americans simply accept that as a fact. Like death and taxes, we shrug over the fact that a certain number of students will not be served by regular schools; that some will always fall through the cracks.

I don't believe it has to be that way. Certainly, some students will struggle, even in our system, but to give up on them is a terrible thing. I wasn't ready to give up on any of them. Accepting the notion that "some students will always fail" seems like an appalling cop-out to me. As long as teachers teach only one way, and don't take into consideration the strengths and weaknesses of each child, then yes, many students will continue to fail to reach their full potential. But, if we chose to have ten or fifteen approaches rather than just one, we could do a much better job of getting each child engaged.

The Education Police

A teacher from a town near Sacramento, to whom I promised anonymity in this book, recently told me the following story. "In our district," she said with some disgust, "the district office actually sends a representative to each class to insure that the teacher is teaching from a specific page in a specific book on a specific date." This teacher, who also served as a union representative, became increasingly animated as she went on with her story. "Can you imagine anything more absurd than to assume that all the children of a certain age in California can and will learn at exactly the same rate?" she said, shaking her head. "It is terrible because if you don't adhere to their standards—which are handed down from on "High," meaning the State Department of Education, if you aren't teaching from exactly the page they tell you to, you will get black marks against you as a teacher. It's like the Spanish Inquisition. How are you going to keep teachers motivated when you force them to kowtow to a bureaucracy that thinks it knows everything there is to know about teaching? We hate it. Many of us are considering either retiring early or changing professions altogether."

She and I were working out in a local gym as we talked, and the more she discussed the situations of teachers in California, the angrier she got. "Most teachers are in the profession because we have a serious desire to work with children," she said, pumping some iron with an angry jerk of her bicep. "Most of us bring different talents, ideas and skills to the classroom and we are capable of adjusting our teaching methods to the type of students we have in each class. Believe me, every class you have is different and teachers need to be given the flexibility and freedom to adjust as we see fit. We need to be able to teach! The way it is now, we are simply servants of the state. We must do exactly what they tell us to do and exactly how they tell us to do it. How many people do you know who will stay inspired and motivated working under conditions like that?" She put the weight set back into the rack with a thud and I wished at that moment she could confront the educrats in Sacramento. She was mad enough and fit enough to send them running for cover.

As I thought about our conversation later, though, the image of teachers having any kind of power faded. I became increasingly dismayed because this woman was clearly committed—or had been committed—to helping young people learn and grow into responsible adults, and now she was looking to get out of the profession. We simply can't afford to waste the talents of good teachers like her.

The "OPEC" of Public Education

There is also a serious question about whether the current credentialing process conducted by state departments of education and collegiate schools of education is actually doing more harm than good. Teachers, in large part, aren't learning how to teach, but much like the students in K-12 throughout America, they are rewarded instead for how well they can memorize facts. The premise behind these credentialing programs is faulty. We don't need teachers to memorize tons of facts so they can transfer these facts on to the students. Teachers should be taught how to guide students toward learning how to gather and attain information on their own from the world around them. This should be the primary goal of all teachers, to show students how to become lifelong learners by teaching them how to find answers to questions for themselves from the multitude of information sources that is available to them. When you teach children how to do this, you can turn them loose and they can learn anything. They can continue to be learning machines for the rest of their lives. The current school process takes this away from students.

Let me ask you, who is going to be better served: the student who is required to memorize many of the same facts that the teacher was required to memorize during the credentialing process, or the student who is taught how to find the answer to any question presented to him or her? We all learn without being taught. Few of us were taught how to speak; we learned hundreds and even thousands of words on our own before we went to school. Think of it this way. If the only method of learning is to have another human being teach us, we must always have a teacher around in order for us to learn.

We must set up our schools to help children learn on their own, with guidance and mentoring by a teacher. Teachers should no longer be viewed as the "keepers of knowledge" who pass it down, piece by piece, to the students. Rather, they should be coaches and mentors who help children learn on their own. This is a hard role change for many teachers. Under the current system, they are the center of the students' universe. Some fear lessening this role will reduce their salaries and status. Moreover, the power and feeling of being a dictator is seductive. Power is a hard addiction to overcome.

We send our children to school for seven or eight hours a day and during most of that time they are being blocked from self-learning by teachers who believe it is their role to simply pass on the information they have learned to the students. This method works against the motivation of many children, and many children feel they have to endure schooling.

To break out of the malaise of mediocrity that now has an iron grip on our public schools, teachers must begin to define their role as that of resources and guides, and not the centers of the universe. By the way, this approach is precisely what business leadership experts are now advocating. Companies like Microsoft, General Motors, Southwest Airlines, Pepsi and others have all changed their attitude toward leadership. No longer is the boss someone expected to look down on the employees to strictly monitor and control their behavior. Supervisors and leaders are now trained to inspire, coach and motivate workers, who are encouraged to learn and solve problems on their own.

To equip our children with the skills necessary to thrive in this new business environment, we must teach them to learn on their own. Spoon-feeding them a plethora of meaningless facts, then "testing" them by having them repeat these facts a short time later, is an archaic approach. We need to get our children engaged with learning by teaching them there is nothing they can't find on their own. Of course, the teacher needs to be a primary resource and should continue to lead the learning process.

If you think I'm being hard on the credentialing process, go ask some teachers if they think it makes sense. The majority of the teachers I've talked to have some highly critical things to say about it. Most agree with a scathing report on the credentialing process released in 2000 by the Lexington Institute, a non-profit public policy research organization in Arlington, Virginia. Here are some short excerpts from that report.

"State departments of education and collegiate schools of education have put in place over the years a system for certifying schoolteachers that rewards process over substance," the authors charged. "Requirements for mind-numbing courses in the intricacies of professional education deter many bright young people, as well as career-switchers, from becoming teachers."[24]

The report criticizes the current system for "barely taking achievement into account at all." The unions and the state departments of education have collaborated to standardize and centralize education more than ever before. The Lexington Institute report calls for a breakup of what it calls this "education cartel," this "OPEC of public education."[25]

The report also points out that "The government licensing agencies, which are charged with protecting the public interest, are effectively controlled by those interests—in this case, the teacher-trainers—they are supposed to be regulating."[26] In effect, the fox is guarding the hen house.

Politically Correct But Short on Substance

Also heavily criticized in the Lexington Institute report is the fact that the credentialing process places a primary emphasis, well beyond even that of teaching skills and mentoring abilities, on cultural and political correctness. "An aspiring teacher typically must complete a state-approved regimen of teacher education that too often is heavy on pedagogical murk like 'managing classroom diversity' and woefully light on intellectual substance,"[27] the report criticized. By the way, I have often heard similar criticisms by teachers, who feel the amount of time and effort they must give to this "pedagogical murk" is useless and insulting. A good teacher, a good human being, will have no trouble being sensitive to classroom diversity. In fact, I find it amazingly hypocritical that the same educrats who want to homogenize and standardize learning to a point where only a narrow band of students are served, will, at the same time, force aspiring teachers to listen to teacher-trainers drone on about how to handle student diversity! The fact is—and I doubt many parents whose children fall under the "diverse" label would disagree with me—the best thing you can do for any child, regardless of race, color or creed, is to engage them at school and to teach them, on an individual basis, how to become a lifelong learner!

A Free Market for Teachers

Just as Adam Smith championed the free marketplace for the creation of better goods and services in our economy, we should consider operating a free marketplace for teachers. If we are going to find the best teachers to instruct our children, then the process must be taken out of the hands of the bureaucrats and the unions. Individual schools, which should include a consortium of parents, local administrators and other teachers, should be given the power to recruit, select and hire people they feel are best suited and equipped to teach, whether or not they have a certificate from the bureaucrats. Each school should be allowed to "shop" in the free market for their own teaching staffs, rather than being forced to follow the rigid and often useless rules and credentialing requirements set up by the education bureaucracies.

One of the most serious problems with the credentialing process is that those who created it did so in order to produce teachers in their own image. For example, before unions and the bureaucracy controlled the process, a prospective teacher's work experience was considered heavily in judging his or her worth as a teacher. Common sense led administrators to the conclusion that someone who had owned and operated a successful business might be able to provide students with a keener insight into business management than someone fresh out of school. Someone who had worked as a lawyer and then a judge might have something important to say in a law class. Someone who won a Nobel Prize in economics might just know a thing or two about that subject.

Today, that entire concept is out the window. Somewhere along the line, the credentialing process, in the collegiate ranks especially, was taken over by people with PhDs. In order to validate and nearly deify this particular achievement, they made it a requirement in most states to have a PhD before you can teach a class. This is utterly ridiculous. It is self-aggrandizement in an ivory tower setting. Who wins? People with PhDs. Who loses? The students and the highly motivated and talented people who would like to teach, but who have spent their time working in their field rather than becoming a career student.

At the same time, the list of those who can teach in our K-12 schools is equally narrow. Here is a list, for example, of people who *cannot* teach in most public schools. They don't, you see, have a proper credential. By the way, you might ask the principal of your local public school if any of these people would be allowed to teach your children.

> Superior Court Justice, Sandra Day O'Connor
> Microsoft founder, Bill Gates
> Film producer Steven Spielberg,
> Governor of California, Arnold Schwarzenegger
> Musician, Quincy Jones
> Nobel Prize Laureate in Medicine, Leland H. Hartwell
> Nobel Prize Laureate in Economics, Robert F. Engle
> Nobel Prize Laureate in Physics, Raymond Davis, Jr.
> Nobel Prize Laureate in Literature, Toni Morrison
> Best-selling author, John Grisham
> Former President, Jimmy Carter
> California State Historian, Kevin Starr

In most school districts nationwide, none of these illustrious people would be considered qualified to teach our children. While some temporary provision to teach is likely to be made to people as famous as these, to stay in good graces and remain employed, they would be required to take ongoing classes on the mechanics of teaching, with a heavy emphasis on "social justice" and with little or no emphasis on how to inspire and lead children to become lifelong learners. It is an inescapable fact that those in charge of the credentialing process have a strong and well-defined social agenda. These social engineers have placed achieving their collective vision—by forcing aspiring teachers to adhere to their agenda—above teaching our children.

This inexcusable abuse of power has had one positive result, however. It has helped charter schools grow in popularity. Parents see what is happening; they understand what is going on. In one public middle school history class in a regular school near where I live in northern California, a teacher spent years happily teaching her classes that Christopher Columbus was an important figure in history only because he was personally responsible for giving small pox to the Native Americans. She also taught her classes that every year throughout the 1700s Native Americans from every tribe in the country would meet in what is now Washington D.C. and hold a national congress. According to this teacher, it was from the written documents of these meetings that Thomas Jefferson, John Adams and the other framers gained the wording for the American Constitution! Unbelievable! Never mind that none of these events, or anything even close to them, ever happened. Don't get me wrong—I am all in favor of teaching the full breadth of history, including the contributions of all peoples, but this was pure fiction taught to the detriment of all students. Such a teacher would not have lasted one semester in a school where the veracity of her teaching and the quality of her work was scrutinized by the parents.

The bottom line here is that this critically-important credentialing process must be taken away from the unions and the education bureaucracy, which only seek to perpetuate themselves. The selection of teachers must be given over to local control—that is, parents and principals, with consultation from other teachers. The power of the marketplace must be put to work here. The same system of open competition that provides us with better products and services throughout the public sector of our economy must be put to work to serve our children. Education consumers must be protected with the same antitrust laws as other consumers. Is the quality of our products—cars, toasters, shoes, DVD players—more important than the quality of our children's education? It is time to dismantle this education cartel, this "OPEC of public education," and expand consumer choice through competition to produce the best teachers and schools possible for our children.

10

TWO STUDIES:
How Choice Affects American Teachers and New Zealand's All-Charter School System

The following are extracts from two studies on the teaching profession that I wanted to share with you because I found them intriguing and thought-provoking. One, a report written by Caroline M. Hoxby of the Department of Economics at Harvard University in Massachusetts, explains how increasing school choice would change the teaching profession. Please feel free to underline, highlight, dog-ear or otherwise mark up this section; give it to every teacher you know and send it on to the local teachers' union headquarters. Hoxby, who does a brilliant job of analysis, concludes that increasing school choice will benefit teachers in ways, "that many incumbent and potential teachers would like," including potentially higher pay![28]

The second study is a look at the results from New Zealand school system, which has virtually been a nationwide charter school system for nearly two decades. There are some exciting findings in this report, as well.

The Hoxby Study on American Teachers

The latest revision of the Hoxby study, released in May 2000, reports that there are a number of reasons why highly-qualified and talented people often avoid the teaching profession. Among these is the lack of performance-based pay, caused by the system of tenure, which continues to ensure that mediocre teachers are protected from being held accountable. "There is substantial literature that demonstrates that teachers' unions compress the distribution of teacher salaries within a district so that teachers with the same seniority and the same highest degree are likely to receive similar, if not identical, wages," states Hoxby. "The evidence suggests that the differences are too small to make teaching an equally attractive occupation to people with more and less aptitude."[29] As a result, the more highly-skilled teachers are likely to become disgusted with the school system, which does not recognize their elevated talents and efforts, and are more likely to leave teaching and go into the private sector.

At the same time, Hoxby warns that the movement described as the "professionalization of teaching," which is being promoted by the National Board for Professional Teaching Standards, the body that accredits education schools, is weakening the teaching profession. "This reform movement contains an element (credentials) that is characteristic of most professions, but it does not combine it with the market orientation of most professions, where credentials maintain minimal standards and rewards are largely based on how the market values a professional."[30]

In other words, the current system rewards would-be teachers for suffering through the current credentialing process, but not for performing well once they actually begin teaching. Again, this is a situation of the tail wagging the dog. Hoxby states: "In fact, 'professionalization' is a misnomer for the movement as it now stands."[31]

Hoxby's report flies in the face of the song of woe and doom that teachers' unions and the education establishment traditionally sing when school choice is mentioned. On the contrary, Hoxby found that school choice—specifically charter and private schools—has an overall positive effect on the teaching profession!

For example, her studies show that charter and private schools are more discerning when it comes to hiring quality teachers. Specific skills are more highly sought after and rewarded in charter and private schools. "They value teacher aptitude more in the hiring decisions than public schools do," Hoxby wrote. "Teacher pay is less compressed and more closely related to aptitude and scarce skills than in public schools."[32]

As a result, competition between teacher candidates, and between teachers themselves, is keener than it is in regular schools. "School choice will change the teaching profession—particularly by raising the demand for teachers with high quality college education," writes Hoxby. "If school choice were to affect schools' demand for certain teacher characteristics, then it would create winners and losers."[33] This, of course, is precisely what unions and the education establishment fear most. No longer would they wield the power that is now vested in the credentialing process. Rather, power would be transferred to the parents, who would sit in judgment of those who are entrusted to teach their children.

But, what about the teachers themselves? Under which system are they most likely to prosper? The answer to that question is clear. Quality teachers who have the skills and desire to motivate children to become learners will thrive when school choice is available. Poor, under-motivated and burned-out teachers will not. That final adjective is most interesting, though, because I firmly believe that school choice will help keep teachers motivated and avoid the burn-out that so plagues public school teachers today. Here are some additional facts that Hoxby discovered:

> In areas where school choice is highest—where more charter and private schools exist—schools are more likely to retain skilled teachers for a longer period of time. This is because in a competitive environment, skilled teachers are more likely to be recognized. The demand for their services is greater and therefore, schools must pay them a higher salary in order to keep them. School choice most often has an enriching affect on skilled teachers.

> Charter school teachers are much more likely to have a broader work background and richer resumes than public school teachers. Many have held jobs in business, public service organization or colleges. Public school teachers are predominately single-career oriented—that career, of course, being teaching.

> Charter school administrators have had an even wider array of previous occupations than their regular school counterparts.

> While charter school teachers make less than their regular school counterparts when it comes to annual salary, they make up for it in bonus or merit pay or through extra pay for work that extends beyond their basic job description.

About 80 percent of public school teachers belong to a teachers' association or union, compared with 23 percent of charter school teachers.

Incentives for extra work also vary widely. In the public sector, teachers are paid .05 percent *less* than their regular pay for every extra instructional hour they work. In charter schools they are paid 4.9 percent *more,* according to Hoxby. "This suggests that charter schools demand teachers who are willing to put in extra instructional time," she found.

Charter School Teachers Enjoy Greater Control

Perhaps, though, the most critical advantage for teachers in charter schools is the degree of influence and control they exercise over various aspects of their jobs. Hoxby surveyed teachers throughout the country, asking them to state, on a scale of 1 to 6, how much control they felt they had in their jobs. ("1" was no control and "6" was total control.)

Regular school teachers averaged 4.8 on their response, while charter school teachers averaged 5.6 on the 6 point scale. "Compared to charter and private school teachers, public school teachers think they have much less influence over school policy and much less control over classroom decisions," Hoxby concludes. "It is worth noting that, by an overwhelming margin, the most prominent theme in charter school teachers' open-ended responses was "autonomy."

Hoxby's findings dispute the constant rhetoric from the teachers' associations that teachers actually lose control in charter schools. On the contrary, Hoxby's polls underscore what I've experienced for a decade, and that is that skilled teachers gain a great deal more control over their classrooms and school policies in charter schools.

Hoxby argues that school choice can change the teaching profession by raising the demand for skilled and experienced teachers (which includes practical experience as well as teaching experience). It also raises demand for motivated teachers willing to make that extra effort and it lowers the importance and demand for state-sanctioned certification.

The coup de grace in Hoxby's report, though, is found in her summary: "Evidence suggests that school choice would create a more high-powered incentive environment within the teaching profession, in the sense that teachers would be required to have higher levels of human capital and effort in return for higher marginal wages," she writes. "Under increased school choice, less able or motivated incumbent teachers might find themselves earning smaller salary increases than some of their peers. Such teachers might be more likely to leave the teaching profession early. This would reverse the current pattern, in which able teachers are more likely to exit early."[34]

I can only add one short addendum to that powerful conclusion: Amen!

The New Zealand Experience

Many countries around the world, including Australia, Canada, France, Holland, Chile and New Zealand, to name just a few, provide a broad array of school choices. All provide public funding for non-government schools. The New Zealand educational experience has been most interesting because they have offered school choice for more than twenty years. A report developed in 2001 for Children First America, analyzed the New Zealand educational system and drew some intriguing conclusions. The report was written by former New Zealand Cabinet Minister, Maurice McTigue, and Dr. Matthew Ladner, director of communications and policy for Children First America.

In the early 1980s, New Zealand was struggling with many of the same problems we are facing in the United States today. Their educational system was massive and unresponsive and the parents had little influence. By any measurement, the system was not working. The children of that nation were not being properly served. The report echoes with language that could be describing America's own problems. "There was outright bureaucratic capture and little or no performance accountability," according to the report. "The system consumed 70 cents of every education dollar, with only 30 cents spent in the classroom."[35]

Twenty years ago, the New Zealand government administered education through a constricting and ineffective bureaucracy that was eerily similar to what the United States suffers from today. The government made all the rules, controlled expenditures, determined the curriculum and how it would be taught and how performance would be measured. The result was an elephantine mass of rules and regulations that smothered teachers and ripped away their motivation and ability to be creative and flexible in their teaching approaches.

Do you remember the eruption at Mount St. Helens that occurred in Washington state in 1980? The volcano first shook with a series of earthquakes that finally triggered a blast that shattered the north side of the mountain as the forces that had built up for so long inside the volcano were unleashed. I envisioned that eruption when I read how the parents in New Zealand had finally had enough of the government-choked school system that was failing their children. At first, there were earthquakes of dissatisfaction that rippled throughout the land, and finally the bureaucratic mountain that had calcified the education system came tumbling down. New Zealanders did what we must do today—they blew up their old educational system and started anew, with a fresh approach aimed at serving students and parents.

While New Zealand education continued to be funded by the central government, the reforms were daring and effective. All the regional boards of education were eliminated and boards of trustees, which are entrusted with policy-making power, were established in every school. They make all spending decisions, but are directly accountable to the parents. Each board of trustees writes a charter for their school, and each is bound and accountable for achieving its goals. These New Zealand schools are quite similar to our own charter schools. Rather than being viewed as novel alternatives as they are in this country, *all* non-private schools in New Zealand are charter schools.

The role of the Ministry of Education has been changed from the central controlling autocrat of education, to that of an overseer. While it disperses funds to each school, it does so according to a formula based on the number of students at each school. It is also responsible for auditing school performance against that school's charter requirements. As a consequence of its more limited role, the Ministry of Education was reduced to about half its former size. (Little wonder education bureaucrats in this country don't like talking about the New Zealand reforms!)

Perhaps the key reform, along with changing all government schools into charter schools, was that after a long national debate over parental roles in education, parents were given the absolute right to choose their children's school. "The consequence," states the report, "is that good schools with good teachers get more students, less capable schools with less capable teachers get fewer students and therefore, less money and fewer teachers are employed at that school."[36]

Okay, so New Zealand did nearly two decades ago what many of us feel should be done in the United States today. But, let's look at the results. How have New Zealand's schools progressed under the reforms? McTigue's and Ladner's report focuses on this question. Here is what the researchers say:

"Since reforms were implemented, some 67 cents of each education dollar is spent in the classroom," McTigue and Ladner write. Remember, only 30 cents out of every dollar was being spent in the classroom before the change. The amount of education dollars actively spent on students more than doubled! In addition, McTigue and Ladner report that "Parents play the dominant role in the educational choices for their children. Learning has improved, and classroom size is down."[37]

The report also pointed out something I found most intriguing. Overall funding for education took a jump under the new reforms, without a corresponding jump in taxes. The extra money came from the elimination of huge chunks of the education bureaucracy. A decision was made that all the money saved by cutting the bureaucracy should remain part of the education spending. As a result, major new investments were made in classroom technology, teacher's aids, increased teacher salaries and bringing maintenance and repair projects up to date. Imagine! In one quick stroke, the New Zealand reforms eliminated bureaucrats and increased classroom resources! The question isn't, should we do that here in the United States, it's, why haven't we done it already?

By all accounts, the New Zealand reforms have worked in terms of educational achievements. Students are far more likely to become lifelong learners, teachers report a much higher job satisfaction rate, and student test scores have soared. Twelfth graders, for example, scored a whopping 22 points higher than the average in an international math test, which was given to students in highly-developed countries. By the way, twelfth graders in the United

States took the same test. Can you guess the results? They scored 39 points *below* the international average.

McTigue and Ladner revealed another statistic which should enrage parents of American children. This international test was also given to fourth graders in America and in New Zealand. Math is not taught in New Zealand schools through the fourth grade and not surprisingly, New Zealand's fourth grade students scored 30 points below the international average. Math, of course, is taught to American students at that age and fourth graders here scored 16 points above the international average.

So what happened? Why did New Zealand students soar from 30 points below the average in fourth grade to 22 points above it in twelfth grade? Because they became learners! They were motivated to learn! Their "learning machines" were not turned off!

At the same time, American students went from 16 points above average in fourth grade to 39 points below the average in twelfth grade. What's going on here? Can anyone say our system encourages the majority of students to become lifelong learners? "Evidently, the longer American students spend in our schools, the further they fall behind students from competitor nations," the report concludes.

It is time, my friends, for another educational Mount St. Helens, beginning with an eruption of outrage from parents across this country. It is time we created a little seismic action of our own that blasts away the bureaucracy that is robbing our schools of money, our teachers of their flexibility and creativity, and our children of their futures.

11

THE BATTLE OF
HASTINGS

Like all things worthwhile, achieving universal parental choice in education in this country is going to take a lot of effort. Opposition to it is strong and well-funded. Sometimes, it comes in unexpected forms. One thing I've learned in my struggle to expand parental choice in schools is that educating our children has become a highly politicized process. Perhaps it has always been that way, but the issues of charter schools and parental choice have heated the policy battles and pushed them to a new level. I was a total neophyte when it came to educational politics at the time I first became engaged with the charter school concept in the mid-1990s. But, it became quickly apparent to me that the future of our children's education lies not in great theories or debates of scholars, but in the rough-and-tumble of politics.

So far, in this book, I haven't differentiated non-classroom programs from the other charter school concepts and designs. That's because the real issue in school choice isn't the pros and cons of non-classroom programs, but rather is parental choice regardless of the type of school. Don't get me wrong, I firmly believe that the non-classroom option is an important, if not

critical, choice for many parents and students and therefore it must
be protected as one of the choices open to parents. Non-classroom
programs have their advantages, including a greater ability to per-
sonalize each child's learning program. However, I also realize that
non-classroom programs are neither possible for many working
parents nor preferable to others. Because I was an Independent
Study Program teacher when the first charter school law was
passed in California, it seemed a natural step for me to open a charter school aimed at serving those who had chosen to educate their
children at home.

I am including this chapter because I want to show you just
how political educational policies can become. In 1997, after fend-
ing off the CDE's attempt to close us down, Horizon enjoyed two
years of relative prosperity. Our enrollment tripled and then
quadrupled. Thousands of students enjoyed the enlightened atmosphere of charter schools in our district and throughout California.
In the spring of 1997, I was excited to be elected to the California
Network of Educational Charters (CANEC) board of directors.
CANEC is non-profit organization for California charter schools.

A Controversial Initiative

Horizon was running smoothly and all seemed right with the
world. I thought the worst was over for us. Of course, I was wrong
again. That spring, a small and seemingly innocuous item was
placed on the agenda of one of our CANEC board meetings. It was
an informational item involving an educational initiative effort
being supported by a man I had not heard of before. His name was
Reid Hastings. During the meeting, one of the board members
explained that Hastings, who had made a fortune selling a technology company he had founded during the boom times of the dot-
coms in the late 1990s, was looking to throw his support behind

charter schools in California. A relatively young man in his late thirties, Hastings was energetic and anxious to make a big splash. I will not speculate on Reid's personal reasons for throwing himself into the politics of education in California, except to say that after he sold his tech business in the Silicon Valley, perhaps he was searching for some other world to conquer. He had been a school teacher before becoming a player in the technology world, and he apparently wanted to return to education in a big way.

It's been my experience that successful business entrepreneurs are often supportive of school choice and charter schools in particular. Perhaps they enjoy and empathize with the pioneering spirit of charter schools, and perhaps they understand that companies in the future will depend on employees who are lifelong learners. Hastings certainly fit into this category. He was a supporter of charter schools, or so it seemed at the time I was first introduced to his ideas.

Although we had won a reprieve for charter schools with our earlier victory over the CDE's attempt to shut us down, the unions and the state education bureaucracy had managed to contain our growth by limiting the number of charters in California to one hundred schools. This greatly reduced our ability to become a true alternative to public schools. I believed that if this artificial cap was ever lifted, the number of charter schools in California would skyrocket. Hastings apparently thought the same way. He had decided to launch himself into the state's education scene by sponsoring an initiative that would raise the charter school cap beyond the one-hundred-school limit. (In California, any citizen can propose a new law through the initiative process. If enough valid signatures are gathered by the sponsors the initiative is placed on the next election ballot. If passed by the majority of the voters, and deemed constitutionally valid by the courts, the language in the initiative becomes law.)

I remember being initially very excited about the Hastings initiative. Lifting the cap was a step toward true school choice. It wasn't until later; when I had a chance to read the initiative in its entirety, that I noticed a small clause that called for the banning of non-classroom programs as an option for charter schools. I was dismayed and a bit confused by this inclusion until I had a conversation with my friend, Eric Premack, who had been tracking Hastings since he first arrived on the educational scene.

"A Hardball Political Power Game"

"Hastings is playing a hardball, political power game," Premack told me. "He has already talked to a number of people in the education community and he believes that non-classroom programs are a vulnerability that the teachers' unions can exploit. He can't afford to have this initiative fail. It would destroy his influence on the educational system before he even gets started and he means to be influential. He feels that anything the unions could hang a negative advertising campaign on needs to go. I don't know that he is against non-classroom programs personally, he just means to protect his initiative."

Again, it became sadly apparent to me that the welfare of our students was coming in a poor second to the realities—or perceived realities—of politics. Independent study programs had existed long before charter schools were created, but they were always small and utilized certificated teachers who belonged to unions. In these older programs, school districts spent about $25 per student for books and other resources. Districts considered these independent study programs a low priority and merely a means to retain state funding for children who would otherwise avoid attending regular schools. Charter schools, however, changed this dynamic. At Horizon, we pioneered a reallocation of resources so that about $1,000 per year was designated for books and other learning resources for each student. We also developed individualized learning programs for every student and backed these programs with real money. Parents quickly understood the value of what we were doing and so did other non-classroom charter schools throughout the state. As a result, non-classroom programs began to grow by leaps and bounds. At the same time, some non-classroom charter schools began utilizing non-union teachers.

As you might expect, the unions became alarmed and began to seek ways to curb the growth of non-classroom programs. Hastings was well aware of this. He believed the elimination of the non-classroom programs would mollify the unions and make them less resistant to his initiative. Of course, that meant that his initiative would force the closure of Horizon and dozens of other schools that had copied themselves after Horizon throughout California. I wasn't going to let that happen. It was clear that we were headed for a show-down.

Our initial tangle came at a CANEC board meeting in Sacramento when Hastings appeared before us to pitch his initiative. I openly questioned the need for the non-classroom program exclusion, and launched a heated discussion on the topic. I argued strongly that the reason charter schools existed was to provide innovative educational choices to parents, and by prohibiting the non-classroom programs we would be killing off one of the most innovative choices of all. I pointed out that it would be counter to the entire spirit of charter schools. No one took me on regarding the philosophical merits of my argument. My opponent repeated Hastings's fears that non-classroom programs were the Achilles Heel of the charter school movement. I disagreed with the idea that we had to sell non-classroom programs down the river to further the overall charter school movement. I pointed out that about one-third of all the charter schools in California were non-classroom programs. Hastings' initiative would not boost the overall effort to create school choice, it would cripple it!

We debated long into the night, and finally took a vote. We found that the 15-member board was evenly divided. Five members voted against the non-classroom ban, five voted for it, and five abstained. We were deadlocked.

As the weeks wore on, it became clear to me what an enormous risk that tens of thousands of students, parents, teachers and administrators in charter schools faced because of the efforts to shut down non-classroom programs. If the initiate passed, nearly one out of every three students in existing charter schools would no longer be served. At the same time, the unions would gain control over who could teach in charter schools. Certainly, Hastings hoped that by lifting the cap on charter schools, more would come into existence and offer greater choices, but there was no guarantee that this would happen. If charter schools became clones of existing regular schools, would parents continue to choose to send their children to them? I had my doubts. I believed the entire charter school concept would be threatened if this initiative succeeded.

A "No-Win" Situation

At the same time, ironically, charter schools were equally threatened if the initiative failed. California voters would send a distinct message to the state legislature that they did not approve of expanding charter schools. What I saw as an agenda being pushed by one very powerful man was turning into a potential disaster regardless of which choice voters made!

Three years before, I couldn't have imagined myself becoming a political figure, speaking out in public meetings and the like. But, in late April of that year the issue came to a head at a luncheon debate held by the CANEC board in southern California. I had been invited to debate the initiative, and anxiously I had accepted the invitation. As I peered out into the crowd moments before the debate I was shocked. There were hundreds of people in the audience! I was nervous, but able to find my voice that day before the CANEC board and I gave it everything I had. The debate lasted about an hour, with each side passionately presenting its side. Hastings was not on the panel, but he heard the debate. Afterwards, there was a question and answer period and I went upstairs to grab a bottle of water. While I was there, one of my friends came up with a "cat-that-ate-the-canary" look. "Reid Hastings is being raked over the coals," he said. "I felt so sorry for him, I had to leave."

When I went back out into the crowd, it was evident that a significant portion of the audience was highly critical of the initiative. They wanted the cap raised, but felt the initiative gave too much away in exchange.

I wasn't sure what was going to happen to the initiative after that. If Hastings dropped it, he would have suffered a real loss of face since he had spent so much effort to get it on the ballot. On the other hand, he had to know he didn't even have the support of the people it was supposed to help. When he disappeared from our radar for a short time, I felt vindicated and confident that at last the will of the people may have been exercised. Then something happened that I have since used as a cautionary tale against ever believing that politics is not a game to be played on many levels.

A scarce month after the CANEC luncheon debate, where it was obvious that even charter school representatives were not in favor of the initiative, the State Legislature quietly passed a bill that raised the cap on charter schools to an eventual number of 250. To our relief, the legislation did not address non-classroom programs. Our efforts to protect them seemed to have been rewarded. Then, as we read further into the bill, we realized the legislation did indeed have its price, but in a way we hadn't anticipated.

Hastings had apparently appeased the unions by adding a provision to the bill that forced charter schools to hire only credentialed teachers. At the time, charter schools could choose non-credentialed teachers to teach core classes. Although Horizon had always used credentialed teachers, I still felt charter schools should have the right to chose non-credentialed teachers because the intent of the charter school law was to free charter schools from bureaucratic regulations. I felt the mandated use of credentialed teachers was contrary to the intent of the charter school law. I also feared it would allow the unions and the bureaucracy to gain a serious foothold inside charter schools, from which they would no doubt seek to increase their influence and power.

The entire affair provided a lesson to me. We had won one victory because we actively fought to save the non-classroom programs, but we had not addressed the credentialing provision and it slipped through our fingers and became law. As some of the football coaches I worked with used to say: "We didn't do anything, and so it got done to us." I may have come away from the situation a bit wiser, but I also wondered why our children's education should be subjected to such political intrigues. Reid Hastings came away having made his mark. Shortly thereafter, he was appointed, by then Governor Gray Davis, president of the State Board of Education.

12

TRAILERS FOR SALE
OR RENT

When I was a student in the 1970s, life seemed fairly simple. It wasn't always easy as I suffered through classes that weren't always meaningful or relevant to me, but I didn't know yet about the complex world of politics or what it was like to wake every morning and determine what my "strategy for the day" would be. In those days I always looked forward to the afternoons when we could get out on the field and play a simple game of football.

In the spring of 1998, it had been more than twenty-five years since I played my last game with pads on, but I knew, as charter schools marched into their fifth year in California, that I was being pulled into a new kind of game. The differences were that the stakes were higher, the rules less clear and the action much fiercer. This time we were playing without pads and the football that was being kicked from one end of the political playing field to the other was school preference and parental choice. It was a down-and-dirty contest with seemingly few rules. After more than three years of fighting for what I believed in regarding educational choice, I had come to expect the worst from the political process.

In the first few months of 1998, I was busy attempting to get back on track after spending the prior year battling for survival against the Hastings initiative. Things were looking up, though, as more and more parents flocked to our school in search of an educational alternative for their children. We were recruiting teachers as fast as possible. We never had trouble luring top-quality instructors. They were all excited about the autonomy and flexibility they were offered in terms of working with students and parents to develop individualized learning programs.

My friends in the Capitol—how strange that phrase would have seemed to me a few years before when I did not know how closely linked politics and education are—kept me informed on a weekly basis about what was transpiring there. I knew that the teachers' associations still did not like charter schools and, in particular, non-classroom charter schools. We seemed to be a continual threat to the bureaucracy, which felt it had no control over us, and to the unions, which hated the fact we were not included in their collective bargaining agreements. Neither of these reasons, of course, had anything to do with the quality of education we offered students. The only issue that should have concerned politicians, whether or not we were offering a successful alternative to students and parents, rarely seemed part of the equation. Rather, it was about power and money. It came as no surprise to me that despite the fact that parents and many legislators supported us, we were still being targeted. Besides our traditional foes of the unions and the educrats, Hastings and others still felt that the independent studies programs were a millstone around the neck of the future of charter schools.

"You have to understand he and others from the Silicon Valley had been successful in their businesses because they were able to do things on a huge scale," Eric Premack told me. "They felt either you did things on a scale of Amazon.com or Google or you were irrelevant. Either you are a big dog or you were nothing. They looked at the non-classroom study programs and saw no economy of scale there. To them, these programs were Mom and Pop operations. They simply didn't value the concept."

We knew our opponents wouldn't rest as long as the bureaucracy couldn't manage us, the unions couldn't control us, and we truly represented a decentralized alternative to regular schools. This time, though, the ambush came from another source.

Under the Radar

In the normal course of business, laws are created in California through the legislative process. A state legislator either creates a bill, or agrees to sponsor a bill written by some private group or individual. In due course, the bill moves through the various committees, where it is debated and amended before it is either killed or it moves on. This is generally a thoughtful, if cumbersome, process that focuses public light on the specifics of the bill.

There are times, however when a group or individual isn't anxious to have the specifics of a bill held up to public scrutiny. For whatever reason, the sponsor or sponsors of the legislation do not want the issue openly debated. In these cases, clever politicians often fly under the public radar by tying their legislation to the state budget bill, which is a monstrous piece of legislation that sets the state's budget and is passed each year. The budget bill is complex, with tens of billions of dollars at stake. These smaller bills, called trailer bills, are attached to the budget bill like sucker fish to a great white shark. Generally, the shark gets so much attention that the trailer bills are able to swim through the political waters with little notice. This is the quintessential smoke-filled room type of stuff where the "you-scratch-my-back-and-I'll-scratch-your's" mentality rules. This is not a thoughtful process where the public good is foremost in the politicians' minds. Trailer bills, in fact, often represent the worst side of politics, and it is not hyperbole to say they are a direct enemy to a functioning democracy.

Word began to filter down that a trailer bill aimed squarely at shutting down non-classroom programs was making its way stealthily through the legislature. I was extremely disappointed to hear the news, but not surprised. It meant more time fighting polit- ical battles—time that I would rather have spent on our school. This was a serious threat, however. I knew that we were going to have to fight back, and fight hard.

The most visible of the supporters of this trailer bill was Jack O'Connell, a state senator from the Central Coast area of California. O'Connell, a former teacher before he ran for office, was the influential chairman of the California Senate Education Subcommittee. (A few years later, in 2002, he was elected to the California State Superintendent of Public Instruction post.) The trailer bill O'Connell was sponsoring provided for funding of the state's charter schools—except for those with non-classroom pro- grams, which, as I've mentioned, amounted to nearly one-third of the charter schools in the state. These were cut entirely out of the funding process. In other words, he was saying to the charter school community—"We'll give you money to operate this year, but in order to get it; you have to agree to abandon more than 33 percent of your students, parents and schools."

Thirty Cells and a Bell

To this day, I am not certain just who applied the pressure on him to draft the bill. Some of my sources said he had a powerful aide who personally opposed non-classroom programs, and certainly the teachers' unions strongly supported the bill. Most likely, O'Connell shared the reactionary bias of many people trained in the public school tradition—that anything that provided a real alternative is suspect, especially when it didn't consist of, as Eric Premack likes to say: "Thirty cells and a bell." In public interviews, O'Connell has consistently praised independent study programs, even pointing out that James Williams, an independent study student from Vancouver, Washington, won the prestigious National Geographic Bee. "They all deserve our support and encouragement," he told one reporter.[38] Support and encouragement, though, wasn't exactly what he gave to us. While he argued publicly that he had nothing against non-classroom programs, he was bent on eliminating us from the charter school scene. He was playing tough and he was playing to win. For the third time in as many years, we faced a shutdown of our school.

A Face-full of Stadium Grass

I feared our opponents could win this one. O'Connell and the unions were much bigger, richer and more powerful than we were. We were in for a tough fight and needed a strategy to stay alive. I had learned something years before, though, about battling bigger, faster and more powerful opponents. In 1972, when I was a senior at UCLA, we matched up in our first game of the season with the University of Nebraska, a perennial football powerhouse that was ranked number one in the country at the time. I distinctly remember this episode because it was the day I was embarrassed and mortified on national television. I had just been switched to the center position on our team, which, for you non-football fans, meant I hiked the ball to the quarterback to start the play, and then I had to find and block the generally huge, powerful and surly defensive nose tackle who wanted nothing more in this world than to pulverize me on his way to tackling our quarterback. My job was to keep both of those events from happening, if I could. Nebraska, at the time, had one of the best nose tackles ever to play college football. His name was Rich Glover. Rich was a two-time All-American who was as big as a buffalo and as quick on his feet as a politician making promises. He was by far the best player I ever faced. For months leading up to the game, I planned, "strategized" and worried about how I was going to stop him from beating me. Glover was such a dominating force that he would certainly disrupt our offensive patterns on nearly every play, if I didn't figure out some way to stop him.

For months before the game, I thought about how I should approach the game and a few weeks before we played, I came up with what I thought was a clever plan. I figured my only chance was to snap the ball to Mark Harmon, our quarterback, then shove off as quickly as I could and block Glover down low, before he had a chance to react. The more I thought about it, the more I became convinced that my plan would work.

The game was played on a crisp, beautiful, California fall afternoon. The L.A. Coliseum was filled to capacity. They love football in Nebraska and we could hear a huge group of red-clad Cornhusker fans in the stands, who had traveled halfway across the country to attend the game, screaming for their team to murder us. We were also aware that the game was being nationally broadcast and tens of millions of more people were watching on television. And I was being pitted against the best collegiate player of our time. Great. I wasn't nervous, I was terrified. But, I had my strategy and that alone gave me hope.

After Nebraska kicked off, we ran our first play from scrimmage and I was as ready as I was ever going to get to do battle with Mr. Glover. Our first play was a running play and I was determined to execute my game plan as well as I could. I snapped the ball and exploded off the line, intent on catching him low with a block before he could move. In retrospect, it is pretty funny that I thought that my plan had any chance of working at all. This guy knew where I was going before I did. I launched myself at him, or at least where he had been a moment before, and I found only air. I flew dramatically through the void where he had just been, and landed on my head, having blocked nothing but the stadium grass and maybe an irritated worm or two. Glover easily sidestepped my mad rush and nailed our running back before he could take a step. As I jogged back to the huddle, I thought what a wonderful invention football helmets were and how glad I was to be wearing one because no one could see the look of stark embarrassment on my face. It had already occurred to me that this was only the first play of the game! My strategy, which I had thought about day and night for months, was clearly in trouble. I learned, at that moment, what pure panic feels like. Then, as I approached the huddle, I took a deep breath. I knew I had to change the way I approached the game in the next twenty seconds, before the next snap. I had to do something or we were going to lose in a big way and everyone was going to be laughing at my mad flops on national television all day. I had twenty seconds to adapt and improvise.

On the next play, I didn't fly out at Glover, I just stayed where I was. He faked and stunted and tried to spin around me, but I simply side-stepped and stayed in front of him. Throughout the rest of the game, I employed that simple plan. Wherever Glover wanted to go, I got in his way. He knocked me backwards, but I'd bounce back and keep my feet moving and react to what he was trying to do. I did not try to overpower or out-quick him—that wasn't possible. He was bigger and faster than I was. I simply got in his way and stayed in his way all day long. It worked. My teammates played well, I kept Glover out of our backfield and we won the game. Much more importantly, I learned a valuable lesson that day. It goes something like this: To survive, especially when you aren't as big or as powerful as your opponent, you have to be ready to adapt and improvise even in the heat of the battle. It is usually better to do this before you crash-land in an embarrassing heap, but sometimes doing so drives the point home. If things don't go your way, adapt and improvise. I've also found you don't always have to match strength for strength; sometimes it is enough just to keep your feet moving and keep your opponent from going where he wants to go.

I knew that defeating O'Connell's trailer bill was going to be tough. With the unions and the educrats behind him, their team was bigger and stronger than we were. Because the trailer bill didn't face the normal checks and balances as a regular bill going through regular committee channels, I also knew we were going to have to improvise to keep them from getting what they wanted—which was to shut us down. I was acutely aware that much more was at stake in this "game" than in any game I had ever played. The trailer bill was going to be devilishly difficult to defeat, but thousands of our parents had their dreams for their children riding on our ability to do just that.

Our opponents wanted to close independent studies programs for a few different reasons. First, as I've noted before, some people felt that non-classroom programs made the entire charter school program vulnerable to attack. Since there are no school sites in non-classroom programs and no homogenized or centralized curriculum (no "one-size-fits-all" programs), many educators were immediately against them. Also, non-classroom programs aren't as easily controlled by the bureaucracy. They seemed a rebellious and dangerous idea to the unions, who also fear a loss of control. Even local districts sometimes don't like the non-classroom programs, which I still feel is the height of hypocrisy because independent study programs provide millions of dollars for some of these districts throughout the state. As far as I am aware, none of these districts have ever given this money back!

But, there was another reason why we were targeted. I had, by this time, begun to explore the idea of further teaching children through classes presented over the Internet. This was a rogue and scary idea to those in control. "They just didn't like a guy in cowboy boots saying that children can learn outside the world of learning that they themselves created and controlled," said Dave Patterson. "I remember some of those who hoped to shut down independent studies programs saying, 'I don't see how school children can learn anything over the Internet.' This is especially ironic because some of these people made fortunes through their e-commerce companies in the Silicon Valley. They didn't like you or your ideas because they didn't know what you were going to propose next. All they knew was they were losing control."

Our Celebration Was Sweet

With time being short, we had to react quickly. I had an e-mail list of all of the non-classroom program administrators and personnel around the state and I let them know what was going on. They immediately contacted their students' parents, again mostly through e-mail. The Legislature never saw us coming. Within days, the barrage began. Hundreds, if not thousands, of phone calls poured into the Capitol from outraged parents demanding that this trailer bill be stopped. Parents streamed into the Capitol and demanded to talk to their representatives. The poor secretaries simply could not handle all the visitors and calls, nor could aides keep up with the e-mails that filled up their in-boxes. Parents began telling us their state representatives in the Legislature received so much correspondence about the bill that they begged the parents not to call anymore. "We'd call and they'd say, 'Is this about this charter school thing?' and we'd say it was and they'd say 'Stop! We know how you feel!' and then we'd call again the next day, anyway," one parent told me with a triumphant smile.

Outmatched by bigger opponents, we kept our feet moving and simply stayed in their way. Less than a month later, the trailer bill mysteriously disappeared; a victim of too much political heat. It was a victory for those who believed in parental control and school choice. Our celebration was sweet, but short. We had been around long enough by this time to know our struggle was far from over.

13

A LEAP OF FAITH

The years from 1998 to 2000 were marked with growth, expansion and success for charter schools. During this period no major political effort to shut us down arose and we were able to concentrate on helping our schools operate smoothly. The lessons I had learned in the past few years made me realize that to succeed, we needed to build an economy of scale that would help our schools thrive economically and politically.

From an economic standpoint, I began searching for a company framework that could handle our rapid growth. We were getting so many requests from parents to place their children with us we could barely keep up. Parents throughout the state were contacting us with the request that we open new schools or take over operations of existing ones. During that time, I began to look at education management organizations, which had been popular on the East Coast for several years. For whatever reason, they hadn't yet been utilized in California and the West Coast. These EMOs, as they were called, served as operators and service providers to both regular and charter schools. EMOs came in different sizes and shapes. Some were nonprofit and some were for-profit. Some of them handled only a part of a school's needs, such as payroll and other accounting services, however, many serviced the entire business, finance, personnel and even policy requirements of charter schools. Most charged a small percent of the school's operating budget for their services.

The more I studied EMOs, the more excited I became about their potential. I felt they were the wave of the future. By utilizing an EMO, I felt we could manage and operate several schools at the same time, and therefore achieve the kind of economy of scale I was seeking. For example, we could save on books and supplies (per unit purchase) if we were buying for several schools, rather than one. We could save even more by consolidating services such as payroll and personnel. It fit perfectly into my overall goal of getting the most bang for our buck for our students. While regular schools were spending about $25 per student on classroom materials, Horizon was spending about $1,000 per student. Still, I thought we could do even better. Every penny we could save by reducing the price we paid for resources and services could be passed on to the students. It was a thrilling possibility.

At the same time, I knew that the powers that be were not through with us. I knew that sometime in the future we would again face their wrath and yet even more efforts to shut us down. But, I had learned firsthand what a large group of parents could do in terms of gaining the attention of legislators. I was convinced that creating an EMO that could operate several schools would give us the backing of thousands of additional parents. The equation seemed simple to me. The more parents we had backing us, the more likely our voices would be heard in Sacramento.

A Supermarket of Choices

An EMO would also allow me to come closer to realizing my dream of providing a "supermarket of choice" to parents. If we could group several schools under one management operation, I felt we could expand the choices, in a variety of ways, that we could offer the students and parents.

In the fall of 1998, I came up with a plan that although simple in its construction, was not so simple when it came to turning it into a reality. I decided to form an EMO of my own, which I called Innovative Education Management, Inc., or IEM, for short. To avoid future criticisms of profiteering, I made IEM a nonprofit organization. My plan was for IEM to perform the same duties for charter schools as school districts do for traditional government schools.

To be honest, I was a nervous wreck during this time. I had never done anything like this before, but the constant encouragement from many parents and colleagues helped strengthen my resolve. I had built and operated a number of businesses in my life and I tried to look at this as just one more. But, I knew what was at stake. This was going to be the biggest gamble of my professional career. We had the opportunity to serve thousands more students throughout California and I didn't want to let them down. I was nervous, but I was also thrilled and motivated by the opportunity before us.

A New Frontier

My first step was to gain approval from the Western Placer Unified School District for moving our Horizon School under the umbrella of IEM. The district board immediately confronted me with a choice. I could make this request, the board members said, but before they voted on it I had to resign from my position with Horizon. Moreover, they would make no guarantees to me before I resigned that they would allow Horizon to be managed by IEM. That made it a difficult choice. I was still the primary financial supporter of my children. I had a mortgage and was paying off a car loan, just like everybody else. They were saying, "Quit your job

first, and then we'll tell you if you have a new job or not." It was-
n't the most comfortable of situations, but I felt I had to take the
chance. My desire to play a role in expanding school choice was
simply too strong not to take the risk. I knew my only chance to
follow my dream was to do what they requested. It was a leap of
faith, but I took it, daring to believe that it would work. I turned in
my letter of resignation and waited and hoped.

At the next board meeting, my status was the last item on the
agenda. Without much discussion or fanfare, the board approved
my request. I can't begin to tell you how good that made me feel.
I took a deep breath and said a little prayer of thanks. Well, in truth,
it was a big prayer. We had just survived the crossing and now we
faced a new and exciting frontier.

Things happened in a hurry after that. Groups of parents
from San Diego, Ventura (a coastal community just north of Los
Angeles), Monterey, Modesto and other cities in the state called and
asked if IEM could help them organize charter schools. In a short
time, IEM was managing seven schools and more than 7,000 students. We faced a number of challenges along the way. The ideological cores of IEM—individualized learning programs for each child
and parental decision-making—meant our teachers were meeting
with 7,000 students and their parents and selecting curriculum to
service all of them. To a large extent, we relied on computer models to help us through and to keep accurate accounts and inventories
of everything involved with the schools. We rapidly developed new
software and programs as we needed them. Our ability to learn,
adapt and improvise was most critical during these times.

New Challenges for Teachers

In the midst of all these logistical challenges, I remained determined that we continue to develop systems that kept our teachers

motivated and free to teach the way they thought best. We were attracting and paying teachers from all over the state who were intrigued with what we were doing. We had new challenges with teacher training, since they had to learn new skills, including how to determine from interviews and then hands-on experience just how each child learns best, and then establish a plan to maximize that learning.

At the same time, I was faced with huge accounting, inventory, payroll, and resource allocation issues. In an amazingly short time, we built a highly-effective infrastructure to service all seven schools. Since parents had free choice of teachers, we also had to develop a flexible and dynamic flow-chart to keep track of the teacher-student matches.

All of us worked seemingly endless hours, but it was a labor of love because we believed strongly in what we were doing. There were some down-sides to our progress, of course. As I expected, the teachers' unions and others continually took potshots at us as we grew. They tried to convince everyone that our growth was hurting non-charter schools. When that didn't work, they began to accuse me of starting IEM as a profit center. The fact that IEM was a non-profit organization hampered their propaganda efforts, of course, but my salary was still a target. In response, I purposefully kept my salary down. I never made more than the average salary of a public school district superintendent overseeing an organization the size of ours. In fact, we called our friends at the CDE to get these numbers. I felt that as a leading charter school management company we had a message to deliver to the public and I wanted nothing to interfere with that message. I wanted people to know that we were making school choice a viable reality. We were helping to take it out of the theory stage and offering children a clear and real alternative. We wanted most of all to provide hope to those parents who felt that public schools were not properly serving their children.

The Scandal

In the mid-1990s, there were a few isolated cases of financial abuses by charter school operators. In one case, a manager of a large non-classroom charter school in southern California made clandestine agreements with managers of several area private schools to "sign up" the private school students as though they were charter school students. The charter school operator would collect state funds for these "students" and the private school administrators received "kickbacks" from the charter school operator. At the same time, the private school administrators continued to collect tuition from the parents of their students. The private school students and their parents knew nothing about what was going on until one of the students found out about the deal and told her mother. Her mother was Maxine Waters, who happened to be an outspoken Congresswoman from Los Angeles. Waters was furious when she learned about the deal between the charter school and the private schools and she denounced the incident on the floor of the United States House of Representatives in Washington, D.C. (In an unfortunate coincidence of timing, Water's statements occurred during the week of the first National Charter School Conference. It was not charter school supporters' finest hour.) The scandal made headlines across the state and all charter schools received a black eye. The unions and the bureaucracy took advantage of the situation by discussing it at every opportunity as though there was rampant thievery throughout the charter school ranks. In truth, these were isolated incidences, but the damage was done as all charter schools were tarred with the same brush, especially large, home study programs—like IEM.

I never spoke about it publicly, but privately I was hurt by the accusations that I and others were somehow profiteers, seeking to become "rich" under the guise of helping children learn. I had lost my family, in part, because I became obsessed with making a difference, and for the past three years I had been through the political wars trying to keep Horizon open. Now, suddenly, they said I was a "crook" on top of it all. I was deeply disappointed that the unions and the bureaucracy had stooped once again to personal attacks to try to win their case. My only consolation was that I knew if they could have won by virtue of the facts alone—if charter schools and parental choice were failing to help our children become lifelong learners—then they wouldn't have had to attack me, and others, on a personal level. These were, I knew, acts of petty desperation. Still, the only reason I got through that part of it was because I believed so much in what we were doing. For every bureaucrat and every union representative that made personal accusations, there were hundreds of parents thanking us for what we were doing. It was a ratio that worked for me. I went to work motivated every day.

To help quell the doubters, we posted our budgets on our Web sites. Still, the accusation that there were profiteers among charter school administrators lingered, in part, because few people on the West Coast knew what EMOs, or charter school networks, were. From a public relations point of view, we had mountains to climb. In retrospect, maybe a good PR company could have helped us, but we were way too busy at the time to worry about that kind of thing.

We had curious relationships with school districts across the state at the time. Some invited us in and practically begged us to develop charter schools for them. More often, though, the districts saw us as a direct competitor. This made it difficult because the districts had control over whether to allow charter schools in their jurisdiction. This is a ridiculous situation, as I mentioned before. Out of this inherent conflict of interest came the fact that while the district representatives from around the state were most often extremely cordial to us in person, we knew they were highly critical of charter schools and those proposing them, in private meetings. That was extremely frustrating and disappointing. With something as important as education on the line, it seemed critical that we all act professionally. I was heartened, though, when charter entrepreneurs in California and other states began calling for advice and telling us they were using our model for their schools.

Exciting Times

Despite the occasional skirmish we had to fight, these were exciting times. We still faced logistical challenges and there were different problems to solve every day, but finding solutions was part of the fun. We were making great progress. I was literally watching my dream taking form. By 2001, we were serving more than 7,500 students. It was satisfying to know that we had established individualized learning programs for each of them and exhilarating to think that we were helping them to become lifelong learners. The parents were our greatest allies. They were thrilled at being able to play such a vital role in their children's education. Teachers and parents worked as a team and parents always felt they were a critical part of the loop. I heard one phrase over and over: "This is too good to be true," the parents would say.

Toward the end of 2001, I learned that those who opposed us thought so, too. For more than two years, they had virtually left us alone and we had prospered. That, of course, was their greatest fear. Watching the phenomenal growth of charter schools, our detractors became more determined than ever to eliminate school choice and parental participation. It was altogether too popular. They came at us again and this time they came well prepared.

14

THE REAL
"BAD APPLE"

I promised at the beginning of this book that I would tell you the story of our fight for parental choice, and that the story would contain scars, warts and all. Well, I should let you know that this chapter is the "wartiest" of all because what was done to charter schools in the spring and summer of 2001 was damaging and ugly. I chronicle these unhappy events here because while they continue to affect Californians directly, they also form a cautionary tale for everyone in America who supports school choice.

Learning Without Teachers

To say that IEM was not a favorite organization of the unions and the educational bureaucrats by 2001 is an understatement. While I wasn't being evangelical about my beliefs, I wasn't shy in sharing them, either. In my discussions with charter school advocates throughout California, especially those operating independent studies programs, I was happy to find that most administrators agreed with my thoughts on issues such as changing teachers' roles, increasing accountability to parents and our core belief that students should be encouraged to be lifelong learners.

The hundreds of administrators and parents I talked to throughout the state were especially interested in how, at IEM, we had changed the role of the classroom teacher. Rather than acting as "the center of the universe" in the classrooms, our teachers had become mentors, coaches and resource managers. Their goal was to teach students how to learn on their own and become lifelong learners. We did away with the concept that is still so ingrained in regular schools; namely that students cannot learn without a teacher's direct involvement.

You can imagine the dim view the teachers' unions took of this concept! They feared that we were trying to devalue teachers. They feared that if teachers showed students how to learn independently, surely the next step would be the administration declaring the teachers are being paid too much! The unions' intense fear of this scenario is the same reason they are so adamantly opposed to students learning via on-line classes on the Internet. The unions instinctively oppose any change in the educational structure that calls for teachers to be removed from center stage. I didn't feel that we reduced the status or importance of our teachers by requiring them to become mentors and coaches. Most of our teachers were very excited by these new challenges, which included expanding their skills to include developing the personalized learning programs. The unions refused to see it that way, though. They automatically opposed any changes they couldn't control even if these changes were good for the students.

Profiteers and Bad Apples

In the spring of 2001, the unions and education bureaucrats found an opening to attack charter schools, and especially non-classroom programs, and they made the most of it. A San Francisco newspaper ran a story that implicated a charter school administrator, who operated a non-classroom program, in a conflict of interest. The story indicated that the administrator had ordered his school to purchase materials from a private company that he owned. The story painted a picture of graft and corruption, which later investigations did not corroborate. However, the allegations in the article created the opportunity that those who opposed non-classroom programs had been waiting for. They sounded the alarm that profiteers were raking off untold fortunes from charter schools. The issue created a buzz at the California State Capitol. Representatives vowed to weed out the "bad apples" that surely existed among the charter school operators—especially, they said, among the non-classroom schools. To this day I do not know whether or not anything was ever proved but I do know that the school that caused the furor is no longer in operation.

The teachers' union was ecstatic over the development and nodded knowingly, urging the Legislature to weed out the profiteers that they had warned the public about for so long. "Bad apples" became the term of the day. There were "bad apples" everywhere, especially in the non-classroom programs. Although I was informed early on in the process that I wasn't personally suspected of being a "bad apple," surely I recognized that the non-classroom programs were infested with them. Jack O'Connell got quickly into the act. He promised reporters, including Kym Wright, a writer for *The Old Schoolhouse Magazine,* that he would single out and place sanctions on "those bad apples whose questionable practices, if unchallenged, will, eventually, be pilloried in the headlines, and, or, worse, deny their students the quality of education to which all children are entitled."[39]

But, it was O'Connell's next statement that sent a chill down my spine and made it clear what the anti-independent study charter school coalition's spin was going to be. "Either way," O'Connell said, "it's those bad apples that have the potential of sweeping a broad brush of poor public perception over the entire charter school movement."[40]

"Divide and conquer" has long been a strategy employed by generals, politicians and schoolyard bullies. And now it was clearly the strategy of choice for those hoping to erase non-classroom programs from California's educational map.

During the ensuing years after O'Connell's ill-fated trailer bill effort, he and Hastings had been solidifying their positions. Hastings was now the president of the California State Board of Education, and equally as significant, he had recruited former California Assemblyman Ted Lempert, a Democrat from San Mateo, who had been forced out of office in 2000 by California's term limits law, into his fold. Lempert had been a champion in the state's education reform movement during his time in office, including sponsoring a bill in 1998 that strengthened charter school law and made it easier for parents and teachers to start charter schools. Now a private citizen, Lempert was looking to stay in the education field. He met with Hastings, who helped arrange for Lempert to receive funds from a venture capital firm in the Silicon Valley so Lempert could start an education lobbying firm called EdVoice.

Hastings and O'Connell, with the full backing of Lempert and EdVoice, were waiting to launch a new reform for charter schools. "Bad apple-gate" as I called it, gave them the perfect opportunity to kill two birds with one stone. One of these birds was non-classroom charter school programs.

Why Non-Classroom Based Programs are Important

Before I go any further, I want you to know why I think it is so important that independent studies programs be allowed to exist and be greatly encouraged, rather than be targeted for extinction. I've been involved with non-classroom programs for more than a decade and I know they provide a tremendous service to those parents who want their children to learn at home. It's been proven in many studies that home-schooled children are not, as many have alleged, being under-served in any way in terms of the quality of the education they receive. One expressed fear of non-classroom programs, and charter schools in general, was that they would be used by religious zealots hoping to indoctrinate children with their particular point of view. A 1996 study of charter schools nationwide by the bipartisan, independent Little Hoover Commission declared that this fear was unfounded. On the contrary, the commission found that charter schools more often went far out of their way to avoid religious indoctrinations because they were aware of that concern.

In our schools, non-classroom students meet with teachers on a weekly basis. (For the purposes of this book, we are defining non-classroom programs as being programs where students are taught by teachers, with whom they meet once a week, but the students do their work in their own homes and those where the parents actually instruct their children in place of a teacher.) Studies have shown consistently that home-schooled children are more likely to be successful in their careers than students taught at traditional "brick and mortar" school sites. Non-classroom options are of tremendous value to many parents and students who do not wish to attend regular schools. These are all good reasons to support programs where children learn independently at home.

But, there is a larger and more overriding reason why I have been so willing to step in and fight for non-classroom programs. It is for this reason that I include the details of this chapter. I believe that school and parental choice, and open competition between schools, are not only the keys to our economic future in America, they are critical to the long-term survival of our democracy. One of those options parents should have is placing their child in a non-classroom program. Whether as individuals we like the idea of home-schooling or not isn't the issue. The point is there are tens of thousands of parents who do like this option and want these programs to be available to them. I have fought, and continue to fight for the right of non-classroom programs to remain a true alternative and thus to widen the choices available to students and parents. Any attempt at diminishing this alternative is an attempt to diminish school choice.

There are other ways to view this issue, of course. The teachers' unions don't see non-classroom programs as a viable school choice, but rather a threat to the unions' control over the collective bargaining units throughout the state. Less than 25 percent of non-classroom program teachers belonged to unions. Our success threatens union control. It is critical to understand the underpinnings of the unions' opposition because anyone hoping to create or enhance charter school laws must deal with the unions.

The School Site Funding Issue

One issue the original charter school law in California did not address was how charter schools were to fund the construction or reconstruction of school facilities, including school buildings, playgrounds, etc. By 2001, this oversight had become a serious obstacle to charter schools growth. Lending institutions saw charter schools as a risky investment. After all, charter schools could be closed for poor performance and their charters had to be renewed every five years. There was no long-term security and most banks and lending institutions refused to extend credit. At the same time, in contrast to public schools, charter schools were not allowed to issue low-risk general obligation bonds to fund facilities. Charter schools were in a bind. They were growing by leaps and bounds, and needed new facilities, but there was no way to obtain the funding for these facilities. The federal government provided a little help, but O'Connell and Hastings wanted the state to step in and solve the problem so charter schools could continue to grow. Remember, O'Connell wasn't against charter schools, per se, only non-classroom charter schools.

That year, O'Connell sponsored a program called the Charter School Facility Grant Program, which came to be known as SB (Senate Bill) 740 in the California State Legislature. The bill helped charter schools with rent and lease expenses. There were strings attached, of course. In this case, to be eligible for a facilities grant, a charter school was required to have at least 70 percent of its pupils eligible for free or reduced-price meals or be located in an attendance area with a population in the same or lower income bracket. In other words, the money was more available in economically-poor areas than in others. In spite of this restriction, this part of SB 740 was a positive step for charter schools, although it certainly didn't completely solve the facility-purchase or conversion problems of many schools. Nevertheless, it was a bill we all could have supported—except that O'Connell and Hastings weren't finished. They added a "poison pill" provision to SB 740 that, ironically, turned most of the charter school members against it. The language added to the bill called for a reduction in funding to non-classroom programs, as well as forcing non-classroom programs to approach the CDE, hat in hand, and virtually beg for their annual budgets. If SB 740 passed, non-classroom program administrators would have to prove they weren't cheating the state and their own students before they would be given the money by the CDE. The original concept that charter schools were to be an alternative to regular schools and free from bureaucratic control was thrown out the window.

In reality, few cases of profiteering were ever proven. My sense was there certainly weren't any more cases of non-classroom program administrators illegally cleaning out the cookie jar than there were cases of administrators of regular schools skimming or stealing from their coffers. Certainly, I am not saying abuses did not happen. I am just saying that this type of embezzlement and theft is going to occur at a certain level whenever and wherever human beings are entrusted with public money. But, by now the damage had been done in Sacramento. The "bad apple" spin had been spun and the damage done.

In truth, whatever their feelings about the alleged profiteering, the fact was O'Connell and Hastings knew that to pass SB 740, they had to somehow appease the teachers' union. I believe to this day, that the non-classroom cutbacks were the bone that was thrown to the California Teachers Association to lesson its opposition to the bill. We were the sacrificial lamb to be slaughtered at the altar of political expediency.

A Miscalculation

Hastings made an immediate appeal to the CANEC board thinking he could gloss over the hit that the non-classroom programs were going to take in deference to the facilities-funding aspect of SB 740. He thought that most charter school proponents would see it his way. He was wrong. I immediately spoke out against the bill. I said that I felt it was simply a way for the state to diminish the role of non-classroom charter programs and to put what was left of them under the thumb of the CDE. Significantly, the CANEC board felt the same way. CANEC Executive Director, Sue Bragato, called SB 740 "devastating and divisive." She accused the authors of the bill of pitting the charter school community against itself and said the bill "robs Peter to pay Paul."[41] Marta Reyes, president of CANEC, told *Education Week* reporter Caroline Hendrie, that the bill was a "knee-jerk reaction" that should be re-written.[42]

"When the state puts out laws and regulations, they're not doing it with a scalpel, they're doing it with a sledgehammer," Ting Sun, a co-founder of the highly-successful Natomas Charter School near Sacramento, said in the same January 15, 2003 *Education Week* article.[43]

Most of the charter school proponents in the state lined up on our side. But, that didn't seem to matter to the authors of the bill. O'Connell, Hastings and now Lempert had us on the ropes and that's clearly where they meant to keep us. What I didn't know was Hastings had an even more devastating plan that wouldn't be revealed until the last possible moment. This strategy exposed the real reason they were so determined to have this highly-flawed bill passed.

During this time, Eric Premack was working for the CANEC board and had come to realize that despite the overwhelming opposition to SB 740 it was likely to be passed by the Legislature, which was heavily Democratic and influenced by the teachers' unions. Getting rid of the "bad apples" made great press and was too powerful of a spin for legislators to resist. It wasn't until I had a long talk with Premack, sometime after the events surrounding SB 740 were over, that I learned of the entire intrigue that surrounded the bill.

"We had agreed to work with Reid [Hastings] on a bill addressing potential profiteering in July of 2000," said Premack. "Earlier that spring I thought we had time to really work out some meaningful details that would prevent any future problems while still giving charter schools free reign to be innovative. Then, the next day I received a call from a representative at EdVoice who started talking about moving the bill. I said, 'What bill?' and he indicated that a bill had already been drafted without my knowledge."

Premack immediately called Hastings to determine what was going on. Hastings told him an opportunity arose to draft and introduce the bill and he had taken it without consulting CANEC or Premack. "I had talked to the governor's staff (Grey Davis was governor at the time) and they indicated they would not sign any such bill," said Premack. "But, Reid Hastings had the clout and Governor Davis signed SB 740 despite what his staff had said. That's the way that bill got through, despite all of our opposition to it." The bill was passed in 2000 and took effect in January of 2001.

The story, unfortunately, does not end with the passage of SB 740. In fact, it was just getting started. While the bill called for strict regulations on how non-classroom schools must spend money, it was not specific about just what those regulations would be. Premack was invited by the governor's staff to help draft these all-important regulations. We knew the devil was in the details and just what these regulations called for could make or break our future.

"I worked day and night on those regs," said Premack. "We got input from everyone we could as to what was reasonable to spend in certain areas. Because non-classroom programs do not need actual school buildings, there was a strong sentiment at the state level that they didn't require as much money as fixed-site schools."

The problem with that thinking was that non-classroom programs spend far more money on materials and resources for our students because each has an individualized learning program. This was a tough thing for the state bureaucrats to absorb and understand. It did not fit into the world of education they knew—this spending model was viewed as suspicious because it was not like anything they had ever seen before. It was an alternative strategy—which, of course, is exactly what charter schools are supposed to provide.

On average, regular schools spend about 60 percent of their total budget on instructional expenses. The other 40 percent goes to pay for facilities, buses, maintenance costs and administration. Teachers' salaries amount to about 40 percent of the total budget.

After weeks of gaining information from all sides and crunching numbers, Premack and the others working on the regulations found what they felt was a ratio that could work for non-classroom programs. The accepted number was that these programs were going to be required to spend at about the same ratio as regular schools. My schools had always spent about 80 percent of our budget on instruction materials and teacher's salaries combined. We were able, as I mentioned, to spend more on each student in terms of learning materials than regular schools because we had no facility, maintenance or bussing costs.

The numbers that Premack, the governor's office and others developed called for non-classroom schools to spend about 40 percent of their total budget on teachers and the rest on instructional materials, with a small percent left for administrative costs. We all felt we could live with this percentage, although I wasn't thrilled about having our budget mandated by the state. Having charter school budgets dictated by the state was moving away from the idea that charter schools were competitors to regular schools. How could we compete freely if our competitors controlled our budget? This argument held little sway, though, against those who heralded that they were going to end the alleged profiteering.

Shortly before the bill was to be implemented, Premack got a late-night call from a friend in the governor's office, who had also worked on drafting the regulations. "You know those regulations we've worked so hard on?" the friend queried. "Well, Reid [Hastings] is over here re-writing them."

Premack was stunned. He called Hastings immediately. He asked, with incredulity, how Hastings could justify changing the regulations that so many had "busted their butts" to develop. "I just couldn't believe it," Premack said with a shake of his head. "We had done all the work to come up with numbers that gained us support of the state and the CANEC board. I told him we had numbers that would be a win-win with everyone involved. He didn't even let me finish. He interrupted and said, 'We can go beyond those percentages,' and that was that. He unilaterally raised the amount that non-classroom programs had to spend on teachers to 50 percent of their total budgets." What made this requirement so absurd is that students in most non-classroom programs only see their teachers once a week! And now we would have to spend half of our budget on them? It simply didn't make sense.

Unions Are the Real Profiteers

The irony in all of this was not lost on us. The unions, educrats and selected politicians were loudly accusing charter schools administrators of profiteering, yet, it was the teachers' unions that greatly profited from SB 740. In the end, it wasn't charter schools and non-classroom programs that raked in the chips; it was the teachers who received a ten percent raise without doing any additional work or taking on extra responsibility. It was a classic case of "bait and switch," but in this case, the profiteering was done legally.

Hastings' late-night changes served to toss another bone to the teacher's union. Some thought the changes were simply a way to boost teachers' salaries to soften up the unions so they wouldn't oppose SB 740. Perhaps, some said, it was also a way to gain a chit for future negotiations. Whatever the reason, this midnight deal struck non-classroom programs hard. We had always worked off thin margins and now we were going to have to spend an additional ten percent of our budget on teachers who didn't have to do any more work than they had done before! I wouldn't have minded if we would have had the money. But, we didn't! We already had a bare-bones administrative staff so there could be no savings there. I couldn't keep employees if I paid them any less than I did. Besides, all of our administrators' salaries put together wouldn't have made a dent in the overall budget. We had but one choice—reduce the instructional materials and services that we offered the students. That was the ultimate result of SB 740 for us. We had to reduce services to the children because we were required to pay more to the teachers. The irony is our teachers were satisfied with their old salaries. None were demanding raises before SB 740 was passed.

No one liked the idea that there were some unscrupulous administrators out there ripping off the charter school system. If there was profiteering taking place in charter schools, it was to the benefit of all of us to have it stopped. I had already expressed my public support to reforms to strengthen "anti-bad apples" laws, but in the end, SB 740 ultimately had very little to do with this issue.

The lesson to be learned here is that there will always be those with personal or political agendas which overshadow and sometimes run counter to the vision of a free and open competitive education marketplace. We hadn't anticipated our opponent's moves and therefore we lost the battle of SB 740 and it has reduced our ability to provide a better education for our students. It is a law that should be rescinded and replaced by regulations that make sense for our only constituency—our parents and their children. We have hopes that this may yet happen. To those of us who believe in the concepts of school choice and parental involvement, SB 740 remains the real "bad apple."

15

THE DANGERS OF STANDARDIZED TESTING

What if your boss walked in one morning and told you that your salary would no longer be based on how well you did your job, but on how well you did on an upcoming test? What if it didn't matter how well you work in teams and with your colleagues; or how innovative you are in seeking solutions to problems? What if it no longer mattered how well you communicate and work with clients? How would you feel if you learned that the test you were going to have to take was created by an unknown, outside entity, not by the company for which you work? In fact, you learn that your company didn't have anything to do with the creation of the test. Yet, your prospects with the company—your salary, benefits and your very future—depend solely on the score you achieve on this test. What would you think? Would you think: Wow, this is a clever way to run a business!"? Or would you think that the company management had just gone off its rocker?

Most of us would choose the latter option, I believe. Not only would we rebel against this process that clearly does not properly measure our true worth and abilities, we would have serious doubts about the long-term viability (and even sanity) of a company that would do that to its employees!

Well then, why do we think this plan of action makes sense for our children? In the past two decades, the American education system has performed just like this hypothetical company. We force our students to take more tests, at younger ages, than any country in the world. The tests cannot determine whether they are becoming lifelong learners or innovative problem solvers, yet their academic future often hangs in the balance. No other industrialized country even comes close to our hunger for testing and our eagerness to judge our children's academic progress solely on the results.

Yet, it isn't the testing itself, or even the enormous waste of time, resources and energy required by teachers and students to prepare for them that is the worst part of this mania. It is the fact that we have, in the past two decades, substituted test scores for true evaluations of our students. These test scores have become the be-all and end-all measurement of not only our school systems at every level, but tragically, of the individual students.

I want to talk about standardized testing in this chapter because most of us have grown up believing that constant testing is as integral a part of education as school books, chalk boards and the recess bell. Standardized testing has become as American as apple pie, a seemingly unassailable overlay that allows us to judge which schools and students are succeeding and which are not.

"Most Americans take standardized mental tests as a rite of passage from the day they enter kindergarten," writes Peter Sacks, education expert and author of *Standardized Minds*.[44] "Gatekeepers of America's meritocracy—educators, academic institutions, and employers—have used test scores to label people as bright or not bright, as worth academically or not worthy. Some, with luck, are able to overcome the stigma of poor performance on mental tests. But, others do not."

A Holy Grail for Politicians

The truth about standardized testing is that while students have always taken tests of one sort or another, the type of testing and our complete reliance on test scores for student and school evaluation is a recent phenomenon.

Our complete reliance on test scores was, unfortunately, jump-started by the publication of *A Nation at Risk* in the early 1980s. Fearful that we were indeed at risk because of the failure of our schools, politicians raised a hue and cry and vowed to quickly "fix" the problem by making schools more "accountable." Accountability in education quickly became a virtual Holy Grail for politicians and educrats seeking a method of quantifying and controlling the outcomes of our education system. Although it sometimes seems standardized testing has been around forever, in actuality it has only been in the past two decades that test scores have come to define success in schools. Yet, they have quickly risen to such importance that the careers of teachers, administrators and even some politicians often hang in the balance. We now worship at the altar of standardized test scores and through them, this magical notion of accountability. And what does "accountability" mean in modern parlance? Does it mean that schools are being held responsible for helping students to become lifelong learners? Does it mean that teachers and administrators are responsible to the parents for engaging their children and helping them get excited about learning? Does it mean that students are being evaluated on their ability to innovate, solve problems, work together in teams, write, draw, repair, construct, design or perform dozens of other functions so critical to being successful in the workplace?

The answer to all of these questions, unfortunately, is "no." In today's education world, accountability has come to mean only one thing—student test scores. There are huge flaws in this assumption. Many educators across the country have spoken out against standardized testing and more join the chorus every day, but the forces behind standardized testing have proven powerful.

"How has the standardized testing paradigm managed to remain entrenched despite the many criticisms against it?" questions Sacks. "Like a drug addict who knows he should quit, America is hooked. We are a nation of standardized-testing junkies."[45]

A Creature in a Horror Movie

Part of the reason for our addiction is the blatant simplicity—and thus the easy sell—of standardized testing. It reduces what should be a complex, thoughtful and multilevel evaluation to a simple-minded concept that fits perfectly into stump speeches where politicians, complete with furrowed brows and trust-me expressions, thump the lectern and promise "tougher standards" while "raising the bar" and "restoring our education system to the best in the world." To do this, according to those in charge, all we need is to force our students to do better on the tests! Never mind, of course, that no real thought is going into why our system is no longer the best in the world or how to truly fix it. It is easier to affix all of our focus on achieving higher test scores. As former teacher and education critic, Alfie Kohn, wrote, "Standardized testing has swelled and mutated, like a creature in one of those old horror movies, to the point that it now threatens to swallow our schools whole."[46]

Besides the political expediency issue, there is another dominant reason that standardized testing has so quickly grasped a stranglehold on American education. Actually, it might be more accurate to say there are more than a quarter of a billion reasons because that is roughly the amount—in American greenbacks— that the test-makers are raking in *annually,* from the creation and administration of these tests.[47] Not a bad job, if you can get it! A veritable fortune is made every year from these standardized tests and without a doubt, some of that fortune finds its way back into the political coffers to ensure that our utter reliance on testing continues. For the first time in our history, American schools are being judged and categorized, funded or not funded, criticized or praised, reformed or left alone, based on a product that exists in large part because it generates vast personal profits.

The control over whether our schools are accountable and whether our children are considered successes or failures is totally in the hands of the educrats who design and administer these standardized tests. This fact should sound the alarm in every community in the land. Every one of us should rise up in protest. In charter schools and traditional public schools alike, our single method of determining the quality of instruction is now the outcome of tests that neither parents nor teachers have any hand in creating. These tests tower over our education system like some malevolent Goliath. Incidentally, the same groups that design, write and profit from these tests, often create the textbooks required in our public schools. The control this small group has over our children's education is astounding. It is a monopolistic system, with relatively little input from the outside. It runs counter to the American ideal of free enterprise and the understanding that we are a nation of individuals. Standardized testing is the epitome of the "one-size-fits-all" attitude.

There is a final and especially troubling reason that standardized testing has caught on so quickly. As parents, we have been told for decades that we have no role to play in our children's education. This has been hammered into us from a variety of sources, all with their own agendas, none of which includes our well-being. It has left us on the sidelines, nervously hoping that someone will step in to ensure that our children will receive a quality education. Standardized testing, as Kohn points out, has been used as a drug to calm our anxieties. Administrators and politicians use test scores like a placebo, waving them in front of us with all the authority and mastery required to create the appearance that they, indeed, have the situation well in hand and under control. In truth, reducing the education of our children to a series of relatively meaningless test scores is one of the biggest hoaxes ever perpetrated on the American public.

The Damage Done by Standardized Testing

The harm done by standardized testing is considerable. The challenge in exposing this damage is where to start. Perhaps, as always, we should start with the children. How many students—and remember that testing in the United States, unlike most other countries begins sometimes even before the children start school—are damaged by initial low test scores? How many are labeled "below-average" learners? How many, especially at this time of tender self-esteem, are clobbered by poor test results that sometimes even convince parents that their child is "slow"? This negative labeling is a terrible injustice being done to our children and it must stop. Can any test correctly determine whether a seven-year-old is becoming a lifelong learner? Can a multiple-choice test determine if the child is gaining leadership or team skills? Can it properly evaluate innovative problem-solving abilities? The amount of information these tests cannot tell us about a child is staggering. Yet, we judge this child, this teacher, this principal, this school, this superintendent, this district, this state on the results of these tests. If standardized testing weren't so amazingly profitable, it would be beyond anyone's imagination to determine the reason for our reliance on it.

"Standardized tests are too simple and simpleminded for high-stakes assessment of children and schools," writes one of America's top educators, Deborah Meier, in her book, *Will Standards Save Public Education?*[48] "By shifting the focus of authority to outside bodies, it undermines the capacity of schools to instruct by example in the qualities of mind that schools in a democracy should be fostering in kids—responsibility for one's own ideas, tolerance for the ideas of others, and a capacity to negotiate differences."[49]

One point of damage caused by standardized testing that has been well chronicled is the tidal wave of resentment it has caused among teachers. Teachers, by their nature, are generally creative, well-intentioned, intelligent people. Left to their own devices, they will often find innovative ways to teach and most will make great efforts to engage as many children as they can. The key phrase here is "left to their own devices." This is precisely what standardized testing does not do. Rather, it places teachers in straightjackets, telling them what to teach and how to teach it. With their careers on the line, what teacher is not going to "teach to the test"? Of course they will! They have no choice! What time is there for individualized learning? For innovative teaching techniques? For expressing the fullness of their desire to be teachers? They must teach to the test. Their creative, joyful souls are shut down and too often closeted. Many become angry, disillusioned and even bitter. It is as if we don't trust them to teach. Resignation can set in. Burnout is not uncommon. And there is no way to measure a teacher's lack of enthusiasm. This is great damage done by standardized testing. I say, let teachers teach! Let them be responsible for teaching our children to be lifelong learners, not robots trained in short-term memorization techniques. Let teachers communicate more fully with parents and let them help evaluate each child's progress in ways more meaningful that standardized test scores.

I have a friend who was concerned about his daughter's progress in middle school. He recently contacted her teachers, who were surprised by his interest. Not many parents reached out to this school anymore. Three out of six of her teachers referred him directly to the child's test scores without commenting further on the child's development. These teachers were resigned to the testing methodology; they were already losing the will and ability to evaluate their students in any other way.

If Not Testing, What?

I want to make one thing crystal clear: I am not against standards or holding teachers, administrators and school districts accountable for the work they do with our children. We must do that as a society. I am not in favor of anarchy, but rather just the opposite. Only through the union of efforts between parents, teachers and administrators can the best of our education system be brought out. And only through this union can we establish meaningful standards and methods of evaluation. I'm simply saying that standardized testing is not the right method. Even the format of that kind of testing is based on economics, not true student evaluation. The reason that these exams are primarily configured with multiple-choice questions is because the answers can be scored at lightening speed by machines. Thus, multiple-choice tests are not only time-efficient, but more importantly to the test creators, they are cost-efficient.

Breaking away from our addiction to these tests isn't going to be easy. Politicians and educrats love them, and too many parents have come to accept them without protest. Yet, we must summon the energy and courage. Breaking the habit of standardized testing and moving back to (and then improving) the standards we used when America did indeed have the best school system in the world, is one of the most important challenges we face in education.

"The standardization movement is not based on a simple mistake," writes Meier. "It rests on deep assumptions about the goals of education and the proper exercise of authority in the making of decisions—assumptions we ought to reject in favor of a different vision of a healthy democratic society."[50]

What Do We Value?

If we agree that we do need to hold schools accountable, then the first question we need to ask is—accountable for what? What do we need to measure? And after we answer that question, how do we measure it? William Ayers, a Distinguished Professor of Education at the University of Illinois at Chicago, posed the proper questions:

> I'm all for clarity of standards, for a more explicit sense of what we expect from students. The questions, however, are: What do we value? What knowledge and experience are of the most worth? How can we organize access to that worthwhile knowledge and experience? When we look at this school or classroom, what standards are being upheld? Who decides? These kinds of deep and dynamic questions have never been entirely summed up, never finished....Standard settings should not be the property of an expert class, the bureaucrats or special interests. Rather, they should be part of the everyday vocation of schools and communities—the heart and soul of education—and should engage the widest public.

Perhaps the first question to ask is who should do the evaluations to determine accountability? Ayres is right when he points out who should *not* be in charge of the evaluations—the bureaucrats or special interests. For too long, parents have been told that we have nothing to do with the education process; that it should be left up to these experts. It's been drummed into us to the point where many parents believe it as gospel. Of course, we also have to face the sad fact that many parents are only too happy to give up the responsibility of their children's education. We parents are so busy these days with so many outside responsibilities that we sometimes yield to others perhaps the most important responsibility of all— the preparation of our own children for their future.

We must begin to rethink this abdication. I believe the *"who"* in *"who* should keep schools accountable?" is you and me. Local control must take the place of this centralized, test-making autocracy that now rules our children's educational lives. Parents must get involved to the point that parental consensus drives the direction, quality and dynamics of the classroom. A classroom teacher should be accountable to the parents of the students in the classroom. Administrators must be allowed to make decisions based on input from parents and teachers, not state bureaucrats and the creators of the text books and the standardized tests.

Okay, but there are other questions. For example, what do we value? What should we be testing to determine whether the schools are being accountable? In short, what is the purpose of education? How often do you hear politicians debate this question? Let me put it another way. Have you ever heard *any* politicians debate this question? Probably not. Yet, nearly every candidate for public office is likely to talk at length about the need to "create tougher standards" and to "raise test scores."

What to Evaluate

In my view, the purpose of education is to create productive members of society by creating a nation of lifelong learners. A successful school is one where students emerge knowing the basic building blocks of the following:

➤ How to analyze problems of all types, ranging from mathematics and science to life experiences and human relationships.

➤ How to independently seek and find data related to any problem on any subject.

➤ How to create and devise innovative solutions based on this data.

➤ How to work alone and in teams.

➤ How to successfully apply the solutions they create.

While each parent and community should add their own definitions as to what their local schools should be accountable for, there are systematic ways of doing this. For example, here are some time-honored evaluation methods that were used in American schools long before standardized testing came into existence.

Parental conversations with teachers. This is quickly becoming a lost art as teachers' roles continue to diminish. Many teachers are simply resigned to teaching to the test. Their professional opinions are often devalued by administration and parents alike. This trend must be reversed because your child's teacher should be your top resource in evaluating your child's education. That isn't to say that parents should rely completely on teachers' opinions or evaluations of their children. Rather, teachers should be looked upon as allies and to some degree, interpreters of how each child is progressing. After all, teachers watch your child learn for dozens of hours every week. For example, they know—or should know (and whether they do know should be part of the accountability testing)—how your child's mental and emotional state is progressing throughout the school year. Can emotional growth be evaluated on a standardized test? Of course not. Yet, this is a critically important part of any child's development. Accountable teachers will have observed these things. Yet, how many parents, today, avail themselves of what these teachers have learned about their child? Teachers, in the right system, are a wealth of knowledge about each child and should have the ability to communicate this knowledge, in constructive ways, to the parents. All evaluations of students' progress should begin with conversations with their teachers.

Performance assessments. These assessments evaluate not so much what children retain through memorization, but what they can do in terms of problem-solving. Students actually demonstrate doing something. They may design and conduct an experiment, speak a foreign language, discuss a book, give a speech, solve a math problem, interpret an historical event or do any of a number of other things. What teachers and parents should look for is the student's ability to learn on his or her own. Students need to know where and how to find answers to questions and problems and then how to apply that information in a way that provides workable solutions. Performance assessments are excellent ways for parents to witness firsthand how their children are progressing toward becoming lifelong learners.

Portfolios. Periodically, students should show off a collection of their school work to their parents. The collection should be constructed, with the teacher's guidance if necessary, in such a way that it shows the growth and the thinking process of the student. This is a time for celebration of this work and for setting new goals.

Testing. I believe testing—even standardized testing—does play a role in the evaluation process. But test scores should be used as general evaluation tools, as indicators of trends and directional markers—*not as the sole judgment to be levied against each individual student!* I am far from alone in thinking this way. A 1999 Phi Delta Kappa/Gallup Poll indicated that only 27 percent of the parents surveyed across the country picked standardized test scores as the most important evaluation tool in terms of holding schools accountable. The top choice of parents—more than 33 percent chose this as the most important indicator—was the quality of the students' portfolio—examples of their work. The balance was divided between letter grades and written observations by teachers.[51] What is conspicuously missing in this survey is the importance of parental conversations with the teachers. This critical exchange has almost dropped out of sight as an evaluation tool. In my schools, we highly value the constant communication between teacher and parent. Both greatly benefit, but the greatest benefit of this communication is to the students' learning and growth process.

A final criticism I have about tests is I do not believe they are helpful—indeed they can cause great harm—to younger children. In America, we test, teach and test some more so that by the time our children are nine years old they are veterans of the testing process. New Zealand, in contrast, does not even teach math until the fourth grade. Yet, by the twelfth grade, New Zealand students, who undergo only evaluative testing on relatively rare occasions, far outscore American students in almost every subject, including math.[52] By every measure you want to use, it is clear that those who believe that the "toughening of standards" and increased testing will automatically improve our schools are badly mistaken. This hasn't happened in twenty years, and it will not happen.

Community Evaluations

I don't have all the answers in terms of the exact processes by which we should evaluate and hold schools accountable. If I did, my ideas would simply be another form of centralized testing. The point here is that each community should be given the freedom to evaluate its own local schools. Thus, the evaluation tools will vary from community to community. As my kids used to say, "Hey, don't freak out about this." It isn't anarchy, it isn't losing control. This is about trusting Americans to know what is best for Americans. It is about freedom of choice. This is about trusting ourselves again, rather than some nameless, faceless group of "education experts" who make huge profits from telling us how smart or stupid they think our children are. This is about taking back our schools. If this idea of local control does freak you out, just remember that for most of America's history—including the long period when our school system was the best in the world— our schools were locally-controlled and largely parent-driven. Standardized testing has only been the be-all and end-all in education for the past twenty years and during that time American schools have trailed badly in world-wide competition.

It is time for all of us—parents, teachers and local administrators—to work together to take back our schools, for our children's sake. We must believe in ourselves and accept the responsibility for creating environments where our children are encouraged to become lifelong learners. As Meier writes, "The solution to the problems we face in democracy is more democracy."[53]

16

WHY WE MUST TRUST PARENTS

During the last ten years, I've talked to thousands of parents about the importance of parent-driven schools. In these discussions, two questions always arise. The first is obvious and easily articulated. Parents are curious about how charter schools are held accountable for their performance. The second question, though, usually doesn't come to the surface right away; rather, it circles around in the back of people's minds creating anxiety until I bring it out in the open in our discussion. That question, and its subsets, usually goes something like this: "Can parents throughout America be trusted? Do they know enough about educating their children to have teachers and schools accountable to them? Shouldn't this power be left in the hands of education "experts" and bureaucrats?"

This chapter is dedicated to answering these questions.

The Multidirectional Accountability of Charter Schools

Let me start by addressing the accountability question. It is an important one because those who are not familiar with charter schools need to be reassured that this isn't the Wild, Wild West where gun-toting anarchists or religious cultists can start their own schools in which they can indoctrinate their children with antisocial beliefs. As those who are familiar with charter schools will tell you, nothing could be farther from the truth. Charter schools are, in fact, subjected more vigorously to a wider variety of checks and balances than are regular schools. It all starts with the charter, itself, of course. Schools must live up to the promises in their charters or they can be shut down by the state, the school districts, or whatever entity granted their charter. Moreover, if charter schools do not serve their students, parents can take their children out of that school—something that is not so easily done in regular schools. Ultimately, if enough parents choose to remove their children, the charter school will not survive financially. Charter schools must also be accountable to teachers, vendors, administrators and to the community. Here is a closer look at what some educators call the "multidirectional accountability" of charter schools.

Charter Authorizers

These authorizers are the entities that grant the original charter for the school. In California, these are the local school districts, but in other states universities and other institutions can approve school charters. These authorizers monitor each charter school to ensure that it is following the guidelines in the charter. Noncompliance with the charter or state regulations can result in revocation of the charter and closure of the school. The authorizers also release the public funds to the school; handle the resolution of complaints against the school, and decide whether to renew the charter when the school's term expires (usually every five years, though it is longer in some states). Authorizers can ask for budgetary and other data at any time, although it is understood that the charter school, as much as possible, shall be left alone to innovate in terms of curriculum and other processes.

The State

As I've pointed out earlier, California and other states have taken active roles in passing a continued litany of laws that give the state increasing control over charter schools. Charter schools are sometimes audited financially and monitored to ensure that the curriculum and the spirit of the teachings within the school are not antisocial, cultist or in any other way considered dangerous to the state. So far, this has not been an issue in any school of which I am aware. Charter schools are also held accountable for meeting performance goals and, alas, for achieving certain levels on standardized test scores. I believe firmly that charter schools should be held accountable for students reaching performance goals. However, these goals should not be established by the state, but by each school, and they should be articulated in the school's charter. The state's proper role should be to analyze whether the schools are living up to their charters.

The Parents

The charter of any charter school must state the ideas, philosophies, and practices of that school. This is meant to inform and attract parents to the school. Performance is also monitored closely by the parents and this is perhaps the greatest test of accountability built into the system. Charter school administrators know that if their school isn't doing what parents want it to do for their children; the school won't be open long. For example, if the charter states a school will emphasize preparing students for college and the school doesn't do that, parents will transfer their children to one that does and the original school will eventually close. Parents' freedom of choice to place their children in any school they wish fosters immediate school accountability. This does not happen in regular schools where choice is usually not an option.

The charter makes clear promises to parents who quickly know if these promises are being fulfilled or not. Most charter schools offer more individualized learning programs, a smaller, more intimate setting for schools and classes, and teachers who are trained and willing to work with parents in evaluating student progress and using innovative techniques to keep the students engaged and learning. Because charter schools promise parents more, their accountability levels are actually higher than those of most regular schools.

The Teachers

Since salaries for teachers in charter schools are often not significantly different from those of regular school teachers, charter schools must attract teachers through other methods. Most charters promise a more innovative and creative atmosphere where teachers are given far more autonomy to choose the curriculum and to teach it as they see fit. Granted, thanks to increased regulation that runs contrary to the original spirit and intent of charter legislation, charter schools in California are today as bound up in standardized testing as regular schools. Therefore, teachers must teach to the test. Yet, teachers in charter schools will tell you they are still given more autonomy over their work. This is a key reason why Horizon never struggled to find great teachers for our schools. Our teachers love the freedom our schools provide and the control they have over their own work. The accountability works both ways, of course. Teachers must perform effectively, with a clear understanding of the goals embedded in the school's charter, or risk losing their positions. At the same time, teachers must also be accountable to the students and the parents. This is the case in our schools, where parents are free to choose teachers for their children and where teachers are paid based on how many students choose to take their classes. Again, these checks and balances—this type of accountability—do not exist in regular schools.

The Vendors

Unlike most public schools, charter schools are not limited to a "recommended" list of text books. We can choose from hundreds of vendors. We have more than 700 vendors listed on our Web site, all of which are available to parents. Of course, we help parents choose, if they want our help, and we will even select the entire curriculum for their child if they request it. This creative competition allows charter schools to select from a far wider selection of books, resources, technology and services. At the same time, charter schools must handle budgetary issues efficiently so vendors are paid on time or risk losing suppliers.

Some charter schools, faced with this tapestry of expectations, have not made the grade. A small percentage has failed, just as the creators of the charter laws expected. Most have failed because of poor fiscal management. Charter schools are part of the free enterprise system. They innovate, excel, and otherwise please their customers—the students, parents and the authorizers—or they lose their customers and go out of business. They operate under the same rules as any other business in the private enterprise system. Because a small percentage of charter schools have failed does not mean the system is flawed. On the contrary—*some were expected to fail!* Their failure proves the system of accountability is working.

Communication Lines Down

One of the primary reasons charter schools were created was to spur regular schools to excel in order to compete. Charter schools are expected to lead in terms of innovation in education. The excitement behind the charter school laws stemmed from the belief that the successful innovations they developed would quickly be duplicated within regular schools. Thus, all children benefit from the new techniques proven successful in charter schools. To date, though, this hasn't happened to the extent that it should. The problem is poor communication between regular school and charter school administrators. Charter schools throughout California and the country have pioneered some innovative programs that are highly successful. Yet, it is as if we operate in a vacuum. We are ignored, for the most part, by the regular schools, even though we are more than willing to share our programs with them. Whether this barrier has been thrown up by the teachers' unions, or whether it is simply a poor communication network between schools, this part of the charter school dream is not working well. I would love to see the olive branch extended between charter and regular schools with both sides willingly sharing information about how best to teach our children. We can learn from each others' successes and failures so that all children can benefit.

As it stands, the state departments of education have a wonderful opportunity to step in and facilitate this type of communication. If they don't, the school administrators themselves should work to form committees or groups that work together to freely trade information. There is no reason, as far as I can see, for each school to reinvent the wheel. There is much to be gained by opening up these avenues of communication.

Why We Can Trust Parents

Not long ago I was at a school conference in northern California and was approached by a woman in her early 40s. She had three children in public schools and she wanted to talk to me about the dissatisfaction she was feeling about her children's education. "It's like our schools have no direction other than to drive our kids to get higher scores on the state tests," she said. "I really can't figure out who is in control and who is making the decisions about what and how our kids should be learning."

I listened for awhile, and then I asked her who she thought should be in control. That stopped her for a moment. "I'm not sure," she finally answered. "What about the parents, don't they know what is best for their own children?" I asked. A cloud of doubt passed across her face. "Well, yes, that's true for most of the parents I know, but I guess I am concerned about all the parents who don't care about their children. What about them? I'd be afraid to put them in charge."

I appreciated her honesty because her statement summed up an often unspoken fear that many people have when I talk about giving control of schools back to the parents. They wonder, can parents handle such an awesome responsibility? Rather than open up our educations system to competitive market forces, wouldn't it be better to leave control of our children's education to the monopoly of education "experts"? After all, don't they know better than we do how our children should think and act?

I think you know what my answer is to those questions. I am not saying that we parents have all the answers and know exactly the right techniques and curriculum to use to best educate our children. Education, at its most effective, is a team effort. Parents must share with teachers all they know about how their child learns. Teachers must consult with counselors, education experts, test book creators, school boards, and administrators to create a curriculum that best suits their students. Administrators and politicians must consult each other to make sure the funding is available to meet the teachers' needs. When I advocate for parental control of schools, I am not saying the parents should run the show from top to bottom. Each entity has an important role to play. Teachers' unions can play a critical role as facilitators of the communications that need to go on between teachers, administrators, and state-level officials. There is a tremendous amount of wisdom inherent in all these levels of education and we must create an environment where this wisdom can be shared easily without power struggles. That can be done if the ultimate power—the ultimate accountability—is in the hands of the parents.

Local schools should be allowed far more autonomy than now exists, with parents' wishes given top billing. Those who are afraid that parents can't handle this type of responsibility must realize that parents operated in this role—the driver's seat, so to speak—for nearly two hundred years in this country. During that time American education was the envy of the world.

Parent-driven schools represent a system with checks and balances that are representative of our own democracy. In the current public school system, the autocracy of the state and federal governments has all but eliminated these checks and balances. The authorities at the top crack the whip and the rest of us, from the administrators on down to the parents, jump. Teachers teach to the test and we judge our own children solely by how well they score on standardized tests.

But, what about the deep concern of the mother I mentioned earlier? Are most parents capable of handling the responsibility of controlling their children's education? I believe the answer to this is a resounding "Yes!" To say otherwise, in my view, would be a terrifying abdication of our parental love and duty. As I mentioned earlier in this book, there are, of course, a small percentage of parents who, for a variety of reasons, will not or can not take part in their children's educational choices. In those cases, the school system, as it does now for all students, should make the necessary educational choices.

It is critical to recognize that no one in our education system has all the answers. Each school, therefore, should be free to pursue the curriculum and education process it feels is best. That is why parental control is most important in the marketplace. As consumers of education, parents must be allowed the freedom of choice between schools. They should be given the choice of teachers, text books, methodologies and many other things as long as these are not religious or anti-social in nature.

Charter schools exist because people want that choice. They continue to offer educational choice despite the litany of laws that have been passed in many states to diminish it.

Parental control via the marketplace is critical to rebuilding our broken system of education. It must be fixed and fixed quickly, if we are to continue to compete in the global marketplace. This cannot happen unless parents are entrusted with this responsibility. We must believe in ourselves and trust our own ability to choose which educational choice is best for our child.

17

THE FUTURE OF EDUCATION: HOW WE CAN MAKE THE DIFFERENCE

Ten years ago, when we fought to keep our first fledgling charter school alive, I could never have imagined the popularity that charter schools now enjoy. In California alone, more than 160,000 students attend charter schools, which employ more than 7,200 teachers. Nationwide, nearly 700,000 students attended charter schools in 2004, according to the U.S. Department of State.[54] More than forty states now have charter laws and many of them are planning for exponential growth over the next five to ten years. President Bush made charter schools part of his No Child Left Behind program, and nearly doubled the amount of federal money spent on charter schools in the past three years. He declared the first week in May as National Charter Schools Week and has endorsed the charter school concept fully.

As time went on, I became more encouraged about the future of charter schools because I couldn't see a downside to increasing school choice. I began to hope that as many as a quarter of the schools in California might convert to charters. It seemed like a no-brainer to me; but then in those days, I did not understand the reality of politics. I did not understand the power of the unions or that they would act in ways that are contrary to the benefit of students and parents. In short, I had no idea what challenges lay ahead for us. In retrospect, that's probably a good thing. Had I known, I may have chosen to do something a bit less dangerous than taking on an entrenched educational bureaucracy—like joining the bomb squad or rounding up rattlesnakes.

Many of the charter schools that do exist aren't as strong and independent as they should be. Charter schools remain the target of ongoing attacks from teachers' unions in almost every state. In many cases this has resulted in a substantial watering down of their potential to provide real alternatives to regular schools. Still, there is reason to hope. For example, according to the National Association of Charter School Authorizers, an estimated 150,000 students across the country are on waiting lists to get into charter schools. It won't be long before charter schools can celebrate graduating their one-millionth student from high school, which must be considered a good start, if only a start. Here is a quick look at some of what is happening in a sampling of states:

Illinois

Chicago Public Schools recently unveiled a plan for the creation of 100 new charter schools by 2010. In Chicago, charter school authorizers have committed to unique partnerships with training programs, private foundations, and community and school developers to increase the number of quality charter schools. In some areas, business leaders have been asked to participate not only in the founding of the schools, but in evaluating classroom curriculum. Nationwide, other cities, notably New York and Indianapolis, have launched similar programs.[55]

Colorado

On June 3, 2004, new legislation, approved by Governor Bill Owens, created a State Charter School Institute within the Department of Education. The newly formed Institute has the authority to approve state charters. While I am not naturally in favor of creating more bureaucracy, this kind of thing can have merit if the new government agency aggressively seeks to work with existing charter schools to help solve problems and if it encourages new charter schools to be formed.[56]

Oregon

Far-seeing charter proponents here are attempting to open one of the nation's first online charter schools. The effort, though, was recently halted by the Oregon State Department of Education in a bureaucratic squabble over whether such schools should be allowed. I believe that in the future, school authorities will begin to understand that the Internet has a vast potential as a learning tool. Rather than fearing the influence of the Internet, we should be embracing it and harnessing its incredible promise to work for the benefit of our children. Oregon parents should lobby to have the online school re-instated.[57]

New Jersey

A proposed French immersion school here was among sixteen statewide applicants for new charter schools in 2004. Students in the proposed immersion school would speak mostly French throughout the school and in their classes. New Jersey has more than fifty-two charter schools, serving more than 14,000 students.[58]

Massachusetts

Charter school proponents won a victory in July, 2004, when an effort to launch a moratorium on new charter schools was vetoed by Governor, Mitt Romney. The bad news, of course, is that the effort to halt charter school growth in Massachusetts is symbolic of what is occurring in almost all states. Unfortunately, much of the energy and resources that should be going into growing charter schools into quality choices for our children is instead being spent on political battles just to keep the schools' doors open.[59]

Pennsylvania

In July, 2004, Pennsylvania's lawmakers approved legislation that allowed the state's charter schools to buy, rather than lease, facilities to be converted into schools. They also granted charter schools the right to borrow money for construction projects.[60] Only about a dozen states have approved these critical provisions for charter schools. Ultimately, every state should be encouraged to pass them because every child should be guaranteed quality school facilities.

California

Lately, we've gone backward faster than we've gone forward. SB 740, which locked us into strict percentages as to how much of our budget must be paid to teachers, is just one of a handful of bills that have passed with union support in an effort to hamstring new charter schools growth and operating independence.

In 2002-03, charter schools served 2.3 percent of the state's public school students.[61] Many of us had hoped that number might be up around 10 percent by now, but those hopes were delivered a blow in the summer of 2004, when a bill sponsored by then state Assemblywoman Patricia Bates, which would have given California universities the power to authorize new charter schools, was killed in committee, a victim of pressure from the educrats and the unions.

Hopefully, similar legislation will be generated again in the near future because it is critical that the power to authorize new charter schools be expanded beyond local school districts. As I pointed out in earlier chapters, there is a direct conflict of interest in this system because school districts often feel threatened by charter schools. It makes no sense, then, if our governments are serious about increasing school choice, to allow school districts to be the only entities to authorize new charter schools. Other states, such as New York and Michigan have long allowed universities to authorize and even operate charter schools. In fact, in those two states, an estimated 80 percent of the charter schools are operated by institutions of higher learning.[62] This system should be adopted in California and other states.

Economically-Poor Areas Favor Charters

One of the more powerful political arguments for charter schools has been that they are heavily favored by parents in lower-income areas, especially in the inner cities. Studies show consistently that about seventy percent of the parents in these areas favor school choice because they believe regular schools are failing their children. An early argument that was floated against charter schools was that they are elitist in nature, choosing only privileged children from the wealthier families. Clearly, this has been proven false as charter schools thrive in economically poor urban areas.

Changing Roles

If school choice is to become a reality, there must be a shift in the various roles of charter school administrators, authorizers, teachers, state education officials, unions, and even the parents. If I can look into my crystal ball for a moment, (I keep it on the shelf next to my pictures of Presidents Reagan, Clinton, Bush I, Bush II, and activist, Rosa Parks; all charter school endorsers). Here is how I believe these roles must evolve:

Charter School Administrators—Too many charter school operators feel the less they have to do with the entity that authorizes their charter the better. In some ways, I know how they feel. Many authorizers do not go out of their way to create a partnership attitude, but rather approach charter schools with hostility, as though they are perpetually trying to find them in noncompliance. For our part, charter school operators have to ignore that often-times confrontational attitude and we have to follow every law and regulation. This isn't always easy because in many cases, regulations are vague or not completed. It is up to the charter school administrators to work to have these defined. Sometimes, doing so is a difficult task, but we have to make every attempt. We need to attend as many meetings and conferences on charter schools as possible to stay current because charter laws and regulations change all the time.

We administrators must also be open and free with information about our schools so that administrators and teachers in other schools, charter and regular schools alike, can replicate our efforts (and visa versa), if they wish. It is also critical that we take the lead role in articulating our charters to parents, teachers, governing boards and everyone else involved so that the goals, roles and procedures of the school are clearly understood by everyone. Financial and budgetary issues must be handled in an open and aboveboard process that leaves no doubt about where and how the monies are spent. Charter school opponents will seize any opportunity to criticize all charter schools for the questionable practices of a few.

Finally, we must do a better job of developing methods for showing how each school is being operated in a manner consistent with its charter. This is the true litmus test for charter schools—are they operating in a way that is true to their charters? Too often, the only accountability measure most charter schools face is the rank of their students' scores on the standardized tests.

Authorizers—It is critical to the future growth of charter schools that the number of entities allowed to grant charters is expanded. Universities and other educational groups should be given authorization powers. It makes no sense to place sole authorizing power in the hands of school districts, which have a natural motive to control or even reduce the number of charter schools.

Teachers—The role of teachers inside charter schools, and hopefully within regular schools as well, should continue to evolve in exciting ways. For example, if we are to serve students in the best way possible, we must train teachers how to develop a customized learning plan for each student. We need to unhook ourselves from the assembly-line approach that regular schools now take toward students. The one-size-fits-all attitude that leaves so many children behind must become a thing of the past. This isn't going to be a simple change, however, because the teachers' unions oppose it. Such a change means that file cabinets that have fifteen years of lessons plans stored inside are now obsolete. Teachers should be asked to work more creatively, using a fresh approach each year.

In order to achieve these things, we have to give up our addiction to standardized testing. If we don't, teachers will continue to have no choice but to teach to the test year after year, changing only when the tests change. Our goal should be to create a more enlightened environment, where teachers are encouraged to initiate programs customized for their students. We must get standardized tests out of our teachers' way and let them begin leading students toward the goal of being lifelong learners. To begin with, we can develop modified individualized learning programs where all the students use the same books, but where each child is taught as individually as possible, utilizing the methods that each teacher believes will work best for that child. The extra time this requires will be available once teachers no longer have to teach to the test. This could serve as an interim stepping stone to the ultimate goal of individualized learning programs.

At the same time, teachers must begin to forge new relationships with the parents of their students. At the present time, much of the interaction between parents and teachers in public schools involves some type of conflict. As a natural result, teachers often try to avoid parents. They can do this because they are not accountable to the parents, but rather to the administration and ultimately the school board and the state. We need to reverse this. Teachers must be encouraged to initiate dialogues with parents and these discussions should begin even before school starts in the fall. Teachers and parents should hold open and amiable conversations wherein information is exchanged about how the child learns. Teachers should partner with the parents and become accountable to them, not to an administration that knows nothing about each individual child. It would not be difficult to establish this process of teacher accountability. A start is to require teachers and parents to develop a written plan that describes the teaching process to be utilized with each individual child. Teachers will begin to see their roles as mentors and coaches. Diagnostic tests and questionnaires can be developed to help determine each child's strengths and weaknesses.

Before all this could happen, however, politicians must gather the will to stand up against the unions. Wait a minute! Don't laugh. It can happen. I've seen it from time to time. The fact is we can win this battle, if we work together. All it requires is a little patience, a little noise, some courage and organization and some help from all the other parents who feel as we do.

The State Bureaucracy—The state should play a valuable role in clarifying the multiple and ever-shifting regulations governing charter schools. It would also greatly boost the quality of America's schools by increasing choice through the encouragement of charter schools. The state's actions should be guided by the intent of Senator Gary Hart, the author of the charter law, who has been outspoken in what he hoped to achieve. After all, the proper role of the bureaucracy is to carry out the will of the elected officials in this state and country, not to interpret these laws as it sees fit!

The Unions—Teachers' unions could play a valuable role in helping teachers gain more autonomy over their classrooms by encouraging the spread of charter schools. If they listened to their constituents, union representatives would know that most teachers are frustrated and angry over the nation's total reliance on standardized test scores, which leads to the one-size-fits-all attitude toward teaching and robs teachers of their creativity and self-worth. Unions should not fear a system that rewards good teachers and encourages poorly performing teachers to improve. They should not oppose programs that encourage innovation and initiative from teachers. They should embrace a system that asks teachers to teach children how to learn independently.

The Internet—Online learning is fairly bursting with possibilities for students. Every district should form a committee to determine how each school district can best seize the immense learning potential of the Internet. An open dialog between all these committees throughout the state and the nation should be encouraged so that each district doesn't have to reinvent the wheel. Many degree and certificate programs for higher learning can be achieved through online education programs. Introducing younger students to this means of education will prepare them for the greater responsibilities and flexibility of online learning in college and beyond. Besides, most people end up changing careers several times, and online learning makes those changes possible. We must overcome our initial suspicions and fears regarding online learning and embrace it as a valuable tool of the future.

The Parents—To me, this is one of the most exciting opportunities of all. As a parent, I welcome the chance to get more involved in my children's future. Think about it for a moment. What if we parents could play a real part in the measurable accounting of whether our children's schools are achieving their goals? What if we were no longer at the mercy of standardized tests and instead were encouraged to actually play a valued role in helping schools and teachers educate our children? What if parents were suddenly valued in the process of education, rather than viewed as a hindrance to be avoided and muzzled whenever possible? What if parents were allowed to select curriculum and teaching methodology? I believe this is possible and necessary. We've done it in small pockets throughout the state and the nation. For it to become the norm, we all must become involved.

The Future of IEM—My organization, Innovative Education Management, Inc., will continue to be dedicated to its core mission—the increase of school choice for students and parents throughout California and America. We are developing a variety of resources to show parents and teachers how to set up individualized learning plans. We are working on a process that will allow us to post these interactive resources on the Internet. Right now, charter schools appear to be the best vehicles we have for creating school choice for parents and I will continue to fight to make them more available. But, to do so, I'll need help from all of you.

One of IEM's roles is to help train, and consult with anyone interested in making changes in our current education system by jumping into the political fray. We'll help you analyze your current school board and determine how many votes you'll need to get your chosen candidate elected. We'll also help you determine how much you can expect to spend in such an election and ways you can defray those costs. We are here to help anyone who is interested and motivated to make the changes necessary to allow us to begin to move America's school system back into the competitive environment where it once thrived—and where it can again, if we are willing to make that effort for our children.

The Power of Parents

Ten years ago, when the storm was battering us about in Lincoln and it appeared our dreams for a better education for our students were in peril, I nearly lost hope. I felt alone and overwhelmed by a bureaucracy that was bigger, stronger and far better connected with the powers that be than we were. That's when I learned just how strongly parents can feel about their children's education and future. The anger, energy, creativity and courage of those 700 parents who rallied at the State Capitol in Sacramento changed my life. It proved to me that we parents can change the system. It proved that we can—through the righteousness of our cause and the power of our voices—make a difference. The overwhelming majority of Americans feel the public education system is failing our children. The fall is due to the fact that we have allowed competition and parental choice to be taken out of the equation. This has robbed the system of the influence and power of Adam Smith's invisible hand, which fueled innovation and advancements. We must rebuild the educational system based on the principles of capitalism that made America the strongest nation on earth. Only when parents are considered the primary "customers," who must be served by the schools, can Smith's invisible hand once again play a crucial role.

The system must be changed. We know this. But, we also know this change won't come easy. To make it happen, we must be willing to become politically active. This isn't as intimidating as it sounds. If I can do it, you certainly can, too. Many schools districts are small, with only a couple hundred people voting in elections. You can make a swift and decisive difference in these districts with a little effort. Even large districts can easily be affected by a handful of determined activists. Remember, the chances are great that if you are unhappy with the way your school district is being run, many other parents are unhappy as well.

While I am well aware of the challenges we still face, I am highly optimistic about the future. The blueprint for change is right in front of us. We must wrest the current education monopoly away from the state governments and in its place create a free marketplace where there is open competition between schools for students. We must return our educational structure back to where it was when it was the best in the world—and then we must improve it. There must be parental choice in every phase of the system and as much as possible, we should work toward developing individualized learning plans for every student. Only when we get rid of the "one-size-fits-all" attitude toward our children can we truly 'leave no child behind'. This means overcoming our current addiction to standardized testing, which continues to do far more harm than good. At the same time, we must look to encourage and motivate our top teachers by recognizing them through systems of merit and allow them to become mentors and coaches in the classrooms, with a clear eye toward helping all students become lifelong learners.

There is much we can do to enhance our educational system; we just need the will and resolve to do it. The growing popularity of charter schools—and the bipartisan support of our top political leaders—indicates strongly to me that America is beginning to understand that it is time to make the biggest change of all—the return of accountability of our schools back to where it belongs. It is time to reclaim our schools by reaffirming our belief in the love, wisdom and power of parents.

AFTERWORD:
ACKNOWLEDGEMENTS

As I mentioned earlier in this book, my five wonderful children have taught me more than all my teachers and professors together. Jody, Troy, Charity, Heather and Randy Paul, thank you for a lifetime of joy, elation, angst, worry and wonder. Without your love and energy and support, this book could not have been written.

I want to take a final moment here and acknowledge some of the people who helped me understand, at a deep level, the importance of competition and adaptability. Most of what I learned, I learned from my coaches since sports was such a large part of my life when I was younger. I wanted to take a moment here and say "thanks" to all of those people who meant so much to me in my life.

Much of my early understanding about learning, adapting and succeeding came during those summer and fall afternoons that I spent in the mud and dirt of the football fields at El Dorado High School in Placerville, California, and later at UCLA.

At UCLA, especially, I had to continually adapt—to learn new positions and skills—in order to stay on the team. I had to learn these things quickly and seamlessly and under great pressure and public scrutiny.

As a freshman fullback, in my first contact drills at UCLA, I was told to block Floyd Reese, an All-American defensive tackle. The fact that I wasn't demolished during these drills was a wonder. Floyd was a fierce and great player. But, he was one of the sport's true gentlemen as well, and maybe he took a bit of pity on me— although it didn't feel like it at the time. Floyd is now the General Manager of the Tennessee Titans professional football team and I wish him well.

My sophomore year I was switched from fullback to playing the position of offensive pulling guard, which required completely different skills. I had to learn fast or get killed by the defensive guys trying to run over me to get to our ball-carrier. Helping me make that change were the offense line coaches, Bob McKittrick, who later became the long-time offense line coach for the San Francisco 49ers', and Tony Kopay.

Our coach, Tommy Prothro, left UCLA to coach the then Los Angeles Rams in my junior year. Pepper Rodgers, from the University of Kansas, became our new coach. He brought with him an assistant coach, Terry Donahue, who had once been a defensive tackle at UCLA. Terry coached my position and helped me improve and learn. At the season's end, I received the team's Most Improved Player Award. My improvement was due in part to Terry's belief in me, and in my own willingness to learn everything I could about how to play the position. I played at 215 pounds most of the season and most of my opponents weighed between 250 and 295 pounds, but I won more battles than I lost because I used my head as well as my feet. Terry went on to become the winningest coach in UCLA history and served a stint as the General Manager of the San Francisco 49ers.

In spring practice, prior to my senior year, I was moved to my third position. I was asked to play center. Our quarterback, at the time, was Mark Harmon. Mark, who went on to become a television and film star, acting in some well-received movies like *The Presidio*, with Sean Connery, and I formed a good relationship. He came from a family of celebrities, but Mark was always down to earth. His dad was Tom Harmon, a Heisman Trophy winner from Michigan University. His mother was an actress in her younger days and one of Mark's sisters, Kristin, was married to rock-n'-roll crooner Ricky Nelson. Mark's older sister, Kelly, was married for a time to John DeLorean. Mark is married to actress Pam Dawber, of "Mork and Mindy" fame and starred in the television series NCIS. (Did I mention my mother once won a Charleston contest at the VFW?)

Anyway, the point is, my ability to compete allowed me to keep company in a pretty fast crowd in college. Mark, despite his royal lineage, was one of the most thoughtful and kind people I've ever met. One Thanksgiving he invited me to his home because I had no place else to go. When I got there, I was surprised to find that Ricky Nelson was also going to be there, along with his parents, *Ozzie and Harriet* Nelson. As many of you probably remember, they also played Ricky's on-stage parents in the old television show Ozzie and Harriet. I was thrilled. I had grown up watching the show and now I was having Thanksgiving dinner with them. At the same time, our team played in games throughout the country and I was able to visit a number of states and cities. I played in the North-South Shrine Game in the Orange Bowl in Miami, Florida and then was selected to play in the Hula Bowl. This was especially fun because we got to stay in Hawaii for five weeks. I was twenty-two years old and these experiences had a strong effect on me. I was just a poor boy from the "sticks." I was quite conscious of the fact that the only reason I was able to do these things was because in this country, fair and open competition puts everyone on equal footing. I became convinced during that time that you cannot separate opportunity, democracy, and freedom from the power of competition.

I spent the rest of that year coaching the offensive line at UCLA. My primary role was as the junior varsity line coach. The head JV coach at the time was Carl Peterson, now the General Manager for the Kansas City Chiefs. Carl and I became good friends and he once took me on a scouting trip to a local high school to watch an offensive line prospect play a high school game. I had never been asked to evaluate prospective football talent, I knew that it was a skill I might need in the future. I didn't think much of the prospect. He was bigger and stronger than anyone else, but he looked lazy to me. But, Carl, who had been doing this for years, thought he was a great prospect. "No, Randy, he's a player," Carl said. I shook my head, but it turned out Carl was right. The prospect was Anthony Munoz, who later played in several Pro Bowls as a professional in the National Football League. It was clear I had a lot to learn about prospecting players!

At UCLA, I played in the land of the giants and although I battled hard enough to become a second team All-American in my senior year, I knew that I was too small for professional football. Besides, by then, I already knew my true calling—I loved to coach and teach. Part of my motivation was that the positive role models in my life, besides my parents, had been coaches and teachers. Skillful, caring people like Phil Waters, Bill Ciccarelli, Gary Kenworthy and Lamar Fairchild, just to name three of my outstanding coaches and teachers, were the people I wanted to emulate. They were the best people I knew and they had meant so much to me as I was growing up. I could think of nothing better than to give back to students what these teachers had given me. It seemed the highest calling of all.

A SPECIAL THANKS TO MY EDITOR,
MICHAEL BOWKER.

Michael's help went far beyond his work as my chief editor. From the beginning, he understood and enthusiastically supported the vision and concepts in this book. Michael, who has written several books of his own, guided its formation with consummate skill. His hand was critical to the structure and can be seen in the easy-flowing style of the text.

As Michael wrote in the Introduction, we hold differing views politically, yet we found common ground in the ideas contained in this book. During the months we worked so closely together, Michael and I came to realize that the blueprint for educational reform contained in this book transcends politics. What could be more important on this earth than the future of our children?

I want to thank Michael for his energy, skill and insights, but most of all, for the friendship we've shared over the years.

My thanks also go to:

Sara Wilson, Vanessa Perez, Rolff Christensen, Susan Self, Dot Wood, and Barbara Jackson for their design work, support, suggestions and line editing.

To Eric Premack and Dave Patterson for their invaluable contributions to this book.

To my first clerical staff members, Dot Wood, Wendy Droze, Barbara Jackson, Nancy Perkins, Carole Haley, and Marcie Lazaro, fellow pioneers of Horizon Instructional Systems, one of the nation's largest and most successful charter schools.

To my fellow administrators, Janet Marsh, Catherine Miller, Nancy Record, Marsha Silva, Gary Clark, Sherri Nelson, Terri Adams, Kathleen Hermsmeyer, Channon Balkin, Keith Alpaugh, Don Brice, Ann Kelly, and Bob Mars, whose talent and innovation skills were critical to the success of our parent-driven schools.

To fellow CANEC board members, the late Sue Bragato, Eric Schoffstall, Charlie Leo, Ting Sun, Bob Hampton, Pam Riley, Mark Kushner, Jonathan Williams, Mary Bixby, Joe Lucente, and Marta Reyes for their courageous efforts on behalf of charter schools throughout California.

To Western Placer Unified School District representatives, Bob Noyes, Roger Yohe, Jay Stewart and the late Dee Wyatt.

To the fabulous parents who supported our efforts throughout the years, Kathy Arts, Karen Englund, Kelli Gnile, April Stewart, and Dave Gleason and too many others to name.

A SPECIAL THANKS to Mike Yadon, the Chief Operations Officer through the growth years at Horizon and IEM. Mike, you always had my back.

To Michael Clifford, whose constant encouragement helped prompt the creation of this book.

To Carl Treseder, Mike Fong, Jay Streeter, Rhynie Hollitz and Jill Paolini, colleagues I worked with along the way who made a great difference.

To the elected officials, Gary Hart (and especially Sue Burr, his assistant), Rico Oller, Tim Leslie and Steve Baldwin for their critical support. And to Presidents William Clinton and George Bush for their leadership and support of charter schools on a national level.

To the Pacific Legal Foundation and to Chadbourne and Park LLP, whose selfless efforts on our behalf allowed us to win some critical battles.

To Arly Capps, my brilliant legal advisor and good friend.

NOTES

Chapter 1

1. Organisation for Economic Co-operation and Development, *Education at a Glance: OECD Indicators* (Paris: OECD, 2000).
2. Caroline M. Hoxby, "School Choice and School Productivity," in *Economics of School Choice,* edited by Caroline Hoxby (Chicago: University of Chicago, 2001).

Chapter 4

3. Ibid.
4. William J. Broad, "U.S. Losing Superiority in Science and Innovation" *New York Times,* May 2, 2004.

Chapter 5

5. Adam Smith, *The Wealth of Nations* (New York: Bantam, originally published in 1776).

Chapter 6

6. Lowell C. Rose and Alec M. Gallup, "The Phi Delta Kappa/Gallup Poll of the Public's Attitudes Toward the Public Schools," *Phi Delta Kappan,* September 2000.
7. National Commission on Excellence in Education, *A Nation at Risk: The Imperative for Educational Reform,* A Report to the Nation and the Secretary of Education United States Department of Education, April 1983.
8. Organisation for Economic Co-operation and Development, *Education at a Glance.*
9. National Education Goals Panel, *National Education Goals: Lessons Learned, Challenges Ahead,* written by Emily Wurtz (Washington, D.C.: U.S. Government Printing Office, December, 1999).
10. Organisation for Economic Co-operation and Development, *Education at a Glance.*
11. National Commission on Excellence in Education, *A Nation at Risk.*
12. Ibid.
13. Broad, "U.S. Losing Superiority in Science and Innovation."
14. National Commission on Excellence in Education, *A Nation at Risk.*
15. John Goodlad and Timothy McMannon, eds., *The Public Purpose of Education and Schooling* (San Francisco: Jossey-Bass, 1997).
16. Herbert Walberg and Joseph Bast, *Education and Capitalism: How Overcoming Our Fear of Markets and Economics Can Improve America's Schools* (Stanford University: Hoover Institution Press, 2003).
17. Ibid.
18. Ibid.
19. Joe Nathan, *Charter Schools: Creating Hope and Opportunity for American Education* (San Francisco: Jossey-Bass, 1999).
20. Priscilla Wohlstetter, Richard Wenning, and Kerri L. Briggs, "Charter Schools in the United States: The Question of Autonomy," *Education Policy,* December 1995.
21. Smith, *Wealth of Nations.*

Chapter 7

22. Alexis de Tocqueville, *Democracy in America* (Signet, originally published in 1841).
23. Nathan, *Charter Schools.*

Chapter 9

24. Robert Holland, *Use the Free Market to Land the Best Teachers for America's Children,* July 2000. http://www.LexingtonInstitute.org.

25. Ibid.
26. Ibid.
27. Ibid.

Chapter 10
28. Caroline M. Hoxby, "Would School Choice Change the Teaching Profession?" (Cambridge, MA, revised May 2000).
29. Ibid.
30. Ibid.
31. Ibid.
32. Ibid.
33. Ibid.
34. Ibid.
35. Matthew Ladner and Maurice McTigue, *School Choice in New Zealand: Sixteen Years of Unprecedented Success,* Children First America, May, 2001.
36. Ibid.
37. Ibid.

Chapter 12
38. Kym Wright, "Spotlight on California: Jack O'Connell," *Old Schoolhouse Magazine,* CDE, 2003. http://www.teach-at-home.com.

Chapter 14
39. Ibid.
40. Ibid.
41 Caroline Hendrie, "California Charter-Funding Fight Hits Home," *Education Week,* January 15, 2003. http://www.edweek.org.
42. Ibid.
43. Ibid.

Chapter 15
44. Peter Sacks, *Standardized Minds: The High Price of America's Testing Culture and What We Can Do to Change It* (Cambridge, MA: Perseus, 1999).
45. Ibid.
46. Alfie Kohn, *The Case Against Standardized Testing: Raising the Scores, Ruining the Schools* (Portsmouth, NH: Heinemann, 2000).
47. Ibid.
48. Deborah Meier, *Will Standards Save Public Education?* (Boston, MA: Beacon, 2000).
49. Ibid.
50. Ibid.
51. Lowell C. Rose and Alec M. Gallup, "The Phi Delta Kappa/Gallup Poll of the Public's Attitudes Toward the Public Schools," *Phi Delta Kappan,* 1999.
52. Ladner and McTigue, *School Choice in New Zealand.*
53. Meier, *Will Standards Save Public Education?*

Chapter 17
54. United States Department of State, 2004.
55. "Chicago Plans for Charter Schools," *Chicago Tribune,* June 23, 2004.
56. National Association of Charter School Authorizers, NACSA Notes, Vol. II, No. 2, July 27, 2004.
57. "Online Charter Schools Face New Hurdle," July 22, 2004. http://www.oregonlive.com, July 26, 2004.
58. "New Round of Charter School Requests is Largest in 3 Years," http:// www.NJ.com, July 22, 2004.

59. "Charter School Moratorium Fails to Survive Gov's Veto," *Boston Herald,* July 21, 2004.
60. "Code Change Allows Charter Schools to Borrow for Construction," Associated Press, July 21, 2004.
61. Edsource Report, *Charter Schools in California: An Experiment Coming of Age,* June, 2004.
62. National Association of Charter School Authorizers, NACSA Notes, Vol. II, No. 2, July 27, 2004.

BIBLIOGRAPHY

Broad, William J. "U.S. Losing Superiority in Science and Innovation." *New York Times,* May 2, 2004.

"Charter School Moratorium Fails to Survive Gov's Veto." *Boston Herald,* July 21, 2004.

"Chicago Plans for Charter Schools." *Chicago Tribune.* June 23, 2004.

"Code Change Allows Charter Schools to Borrow for Construction." Associated Press, July 21, 2004.

De Tocqueville, Alexis. *Democracy in America.* Signet, originally published in 1841.

Edsource Report, *Charter Schools in California: An Experiment Coming of Age.* June, 2004.

Goodlad, John, and Timothy McMannon, eds., *The Public Purpose of Education and Schooling.* San Francisco: Jossey-Bass, 1997.

Hendrie, Caroline. "California Charter-Funding Fight Hits Home." *Education Week,* January 15, 2003. http://www.edweek.org.

Holland, Robert. *Use the Free Market to Land the Best Teachers for America's Children.* July, 2000. http://www.LexingtonInstitute.org.

Hoxby, Caroline M. "School Choice and School Productivity," in *Economics of School Choice.* Edited by Caroline Hoxby. Chicago: University of Chicago Press, 2001.

———. "Would School Choice Change the Teaching Profession?" Cambridge, MA: May 2000.

Kohn, Alfie. *The Case Against Standardized Testing: Raising the Scores, Ruining the Schools.* Portsmouth, NH: Heinemann, 2000.

Ladner, Matthew, and Maurice McTigue. *School Choice in New Zealand: Sixteen Years of Unprecedented Success.* Children First America, May, 2001.

Little Hoover Commission. *The Charter Movement: Education Reform School by School.* Sacramento, CA: 1996.

Meier, Deborah. *Will Standards Save Public Education?* Boston: Beacon, 2000.

Nathan, Joe. *Charter Schools: Creating Hope and Opportunity for American Education.* San Francisco: Jossey-Bass, 1999.

National Association of Charter School Authorizers, NACSA Notes, Vol. II, No. 2, July 27, 2004.

National Commission on Excellence in Education. *A Nation at Risk: The Imperative for Educational Reform,* A Report to the Nation and the Secretary of Education United States Department of Education by the National Commission on Excellence in Education. Washington D.C. April 1983

National Education Goals Panel, *National Education Goals: Lessons Learned, Challenges Ahead,* written by Emily Wurtz, Washington D.C.: U.S. Government Printing Office, December, 1999.

"New Round of Charter School Requests is Largest in 3 Years." July 22, 2004. http://www.NJ.com.

"Online Charter Schools Face New Hurtle." July 22, 2004. http://www.oregonlive.com, July 26, 2004.

Organisation for Economic Co-operation and Development. *Education at a Glance: OECD Indicators.* Paris: OECD Publishing, 2000.

Rose, Lowell C., and Alec M. Gallup. P*hi Delta Kappa/Gallup Poll of the Public's Attitudes Toward the Public Schools.* Bloomington, IN: Phi Delta Kappa International, 1999.

Rose, Lowell C., and Alec M. Gallup. *Phi Delta Kappa/Gallup Poll of the Public's Attitudes Toward the Public Schools.* Bloomington, IN: Phi Delta Kappa International, 2000.

Sacks, Peter. *Standardized Minds: The High Price of America's Testing Culture and What We Can Do to Change It.* Perseus, 1999.

Smith, Adam. *The Wealth of Nations.* New York: Bantam Books. Originally published in 1776.

United States Department of State, 2004.

Walberg, Herbert, and Joseph Bast. *Education and Capitalism: How Overcoming Our Fear of Markets and Economics Can Improve America's Schools.* Stanford University: Hoover Institution Press, 2003.

Wohlstetter, Priscilla, Richard Wenning, and Kerri L. Briggs. "Charter Schools in the United States: The Question of Autonomy." *Education Policy,* December, 1995..

Wright, Kym. "Spotlight on California: Jack O'Connell." *Old Schoolhouse Magazine,* CDE, 2003. http://www.teach-at-home.com.